Writing Every Day

Reading, Writing, and Conferencing Using Student-Led Language Experiences

KELLIE BUIS

Pembroke Publishers Limited

Dedication

This book is dedicated to
- Hazel Boettcher, master classroom teacher who invented the Daily Letter.
- classroom teachers Norma Janzen, Laura McCabe, Sheena Skinner, Sue Gordon, Dinah Phillips, Selina Millar, Katherine Janzen, Kirsten Nowak, and others who have apprenticed in the use of the Daily Letter.
- Dr. Meguido Zola, who taught me the critical importance of a storying classroom as an enabling classroom.

© 2004 Pembroke Publishers
538 Hood Road
Markham, Ontario, Canada L3R 3K9
www.pembrokepublishers.com

Distributed in the U.S. by Stenhouse Publishers
477 Congress Street
Portland, ME 04101
www.stenhouse.com

We acknowledge the financial support of the Government of Canada through the Book Publishing Industry Development Program (BPIDP) for our publishing activities.

We acknowledge the Government of Ontario through the Ontario Media Development Corporation's Ontario Book Initiative.

National Library of Canada Cataloguing in Publication

Buis, Kellie
    Writing every day : reading, writing, and conferencing using student-led language experiences / Kellie Buis.

Includes index.
ISBN 1-55138-169-9

    1. Letter writing. 2. English language—Rhetoric. I. Title.

PE1485.B84 2004   395.4   C2003-907501-X

Editor: Kat Mototsune
Cover Design: John Zehethofer
Cover Photography: Photodisk
Typesetting: Jay Tee Graphics Ltd.

Printed and bound in Canada
9 8 7 6 5 4 3 2 1

Contents

Introduction

We see our work in education as providing a framework for designing a storying time in the day ... an occasion for participating together as a cohesive unit, anticipating and finding learning satisfaction in shared experiences. (Booth & Barton, p. 6)

In *The Art of Teaching*, Lucy Calkins (1986, p. 23) tells the story of Maria who was homesick on the first day of school. On the second day she drew a picture and some letters, and read her brief and simple story to the class. "The girl is sad. She has no friends."

As Calkins tells it, a number of children raised their hands with comments such as "I like your picture," and "I like your writing." But one little boy understood: he looked up and said, "I'll be your friend." As Calkins notes, we need to tell stories, "but we also need to be heard."

Although teachers have long understood the value of sharing stories to effectively teach what is important in the language arts curriculum, many have not necessarily known "how" to nurture a story-sharing community in their classroom. This book outlines how the Daily Letter can be used to create a powerful story-sharing community.

There are a number of top-ten lists scattered throughout the book. These lists are designed to give teachers a range of practical ideas on how they can implement the crafting and sharing of Daily Letters in their classrooms. They also provide teachers with a rich variety of ways to extend the use of the Daily Letter to suit the particular needs of a group of students; valuable suggestions to new teachers on a variety of methods to broaden their repertoire of ways to create and share text; and alternative ways to teach reading and writing than the ones experienced teachers may traditionally use.

This book shares practical ideas on how to build a story-sharing community that binds students, teachers, and parents together; how teachers can use the Daily Letter as a tool to empower their students as self-directed literacy learners; how the routine can be adapted to suit each teacher's teaching style and to meet the needs of their students; and ultimately how to nurture in students trust and respect that who they are and what they do as readers/writers truly matters.

CHAPTER 1

What Is the Daily Letter?

Conceptualizing the Daily Letter

As elementary school teachers, we can create empowered, self-directed story-sharing communities by immersing our students in a wide variety, and number, of shared Daily Letter language experiences . . . but first things first. What is the Daily Letter?

Author: Roahl Dahl　　　　　　　　　　Genre: _____

Fantastic Mr. Fox

They were still singing as they rounded the final corner and burst in upon the most wonderful and amazing sight any of them had ever seen. The feast was just beginning. A large dining room had been hollowed out of the earth, and in the middle of it, seated around a huge table, were no less that twenty-nine animals. They were:

Mrs. Fox and Three Small Foxes.

Mrs. Badger and Three Small Badgers.

Mole and Mrs. Mole and four Small Moles.

Rabbit and Mrs. Rabbit and five Small Rabbits.

Weasel and Mrs. Weasel and six Small Weasels.

The table was covered with chickens and ducks and geese and hams and bacon, and everyone was tucking in to the lovely food.

At last, Badger stood up. He raised his glass and cider and called out, "A toast! To our dear friend who has saved our lives this day – Mr. Fox!"

"To Mr. Fox!" They all shouted, standing and raising their glasses. "To Mr. Fox! Long may he live!"

Then Mrs. Fox got shyly to her feet and said, "I don't want to make a speech. Just want to say one thing, and it is this: MY HUSBAND IS A FANTASTIC FOX." Everyone clapped and cheered, then MR. Fox himself stood up (excerpt from <u>Fantastic Mr. Fox</u> by Roahl Dahl, p. 76).

Badger, badge, midget, fridge, bridge, pigeon, ridge　　　corner, covered, chickens, cider

???? 　　　　　Ask me my opinion on why or why not Mr. Fox is a fantastic fox.　　　　????

Front

I/we have shared the Daily Letter together: _____signature
Messages and Compliments:
_____

Word Study:　　　　　　　　　　　Song Poem or Chant

- - - - - - - - - - - - - - - -
- - - - - - - - - - - - - - - -
- - - - - - - - - - - - - - - -

Chants from the book Fantastic Mr. Fox

"Home again swiftly I glide,
Back to my beautiful bride.
She'll not feel so rotten
As soon as she's gotten
Some cider inside her inside."
　　　　　　　sung by Mr. Fox

"Oh poor Mrs. Badger," he cried,
So hungry she very near died.
But she'll not feel so hollow
If only she'll swallow
Some cider inside her inside."
　　　　　　　sung by Badger

Retell, Relate, Reflect
_____

Back

The Daily Letter ritual has its origin in the morning message, a primary literacy-learning event that arose out of the "language experience" movement of the 1960s and 1970s (Stauffer, 1970). Many elementary school teachers use a morning message each day as a language experience to teach shared reading and writing (McGee & Richgels, 1996). The Daily Letter is one particularly efficient, effective method to teach the morning message (Buis, 2002).

Despite the variations in the names—Morning Message, Morning News, News of the Day, Morning Letter, Reflections, Daily Letter—this informal primary genre is loosely defined as an inclusive, whole-class sharing of the immediate news, concerns, interests, and experiences of the class itself. It is used to consciously attempt to focus the students' attention to particular aspects of the reading and writing of text.

Personal Power and Community Belonging

Contemporary literacy experts (Rogoff et al, 1996, and Cambourne et al, 1999) support the belief that literacy learning should be placed in a broader framework that is neither teacher-directed nor student-centred but a model of "community of learners" (Rogoff et al). A community of learners is a context where a caring community works together with everyone being a resource for everyone else to become literate. There is a mutuality of responsibility, a shared responsibility, of both teacher and student for the teaching and learning of the community. The students learn through assisted social action by a process managed by mentors and apprentices. The community participates each day to share their own important stories, a language experience to deepen and enrich the literacy learning of the whole classroom community. The students share the responsibility for the learning with the teacher and each other. The students share the power with both the teacher and the text.

I was sharing a read-aloud about teasing when I first noticed the sobbing. I shifted to observing the group of Grade 3 students gathered in a tight circle on the floor. It was Vanessa. She lifted a trembling hand to wipe her sadness away.

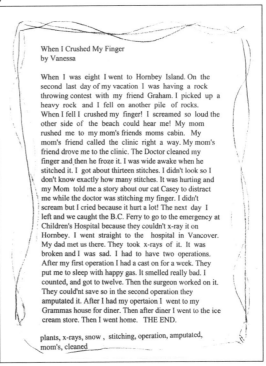

When I Crushed My Finger
by Vanessa

When I was eight I went to Hornbey Island. On the second last day of my vacation I was having a rock throwing contest with my friend Graham. I picked up a heavy rock and I fell on another pile of rocks. When I fell I crushed my finger! I screamed so loud the other side of the beach could hear me! My mom rushed me to my mom's friends moms cabin. My mom's friend called the clinic right a way. My mom's friend drove me to the clinic. The Doctor cleaned my finger and then he froze it. I was wide awake when he stitched it. I got about thirteen stitches. I didn't look so I don't know exactly how many stitches. It was hurting and my Mom told me a story about our cat Casey to distract me while the doctor was stitching my finger. I didn't scream but I cried because it hurt a lot! The next day I left and we caught the B.C. Ferry to go to the emergency at Children's Hospital because they couldn't x-ray it on Hornbey. I went straight to the hospital in Vancover. My dad met us there. They took x-rays of it. It was broken and I was sad. I had to have two operations. After my first operation I had a cast on for a week. They put me to sleep with happy gas. It smelled really bad. I counted, and got to twelve. Then the surgeon worked on it. They could'nt save so in the second operation they amputated it. After I had my opertaion I went to my Grammas house for diner. Then after diner I went to the ice cream store. Then I went home. THE END.

plants, x-rays, snow , stitching, operation, amputated, mom's, cleaned

"They call me four fingers." Vanessa interrupted with a voice as soft and fragile as her hurt hand. The students listened shamefully, more fully aware of the taunting that tested Vanessa's courage to come to school each day. Vanessa's story needed to be told, but not now in the glare of this sad and serious moment.

Several days later Vanessa finished her personal narrative on how her fingers had become crushed. The students remained particularly supportive of her and predictably curious about what had really happened to them. Most of the children did not really know her story other than the ending of it—the endless teasing part—that was the common experience of her present school life.

Vanessa's sharing of her personal narrative was a defining moment for this community of learners. Her sharing of her story in the Daily Letter took many of the individuals of the class by surprise. Suddenly reading and writing became more than working on plurals on the page, or answering questions on far-away times and places. Vanessa was making sense of her life right there on the Daily Letter page. The students shared similar serious situations.

The Daily Letter became more than working on reading and writing skills. It became a time for serious talks about our individual lives and our experiences together.

As a Format

The Daily Letter is a double-sided, letter-size page crafted by teachers or students to showcase their knowledge as readers and writers. The author of the Daily Letter selects the topic and a format of the ten components of the Daily Letter to represent personal learning.

We are challenged to create meaning a number of different ways with the Daily Letter format. With it, we are invited to model what we know in one communication system and recast it in terms of another. We then challenge our students to recompose their ideas in a variety of ways on the Daily Letter. There are many ways for them to represent their understandings, and a students may choose the most suitable one.

When we craft a variety of forms of expression on the Daily Letter, new knowledge is generated for the individual and for the community. Chapman reminds us that "When students can represent their thinking in a variety of ways and discuss the various forms of representation, they learn about their own learning process. Learning a variety of ways of representing allow students with diverse backgrounds, interests and abilities to be successful" (Chapman, 1999, p. 35).

The format of the Daily Letter is not fixed. It is a flexible format to represent thinking in a variety of modes, such as text, visuals, vocabulary studies, poetry, and demonstrations. The format changes with the literacy needs of our students. We can choose new features or create new possibilities for our Daily Letters to stretch the thinking and understanding of our unique community of learners. We can determine the best Daily Letter format to meet the very needs of the community of fledgling literacy learners we share it with.

Each component of the Daily Letter (see BLM #1 page 9) allows students or teachers to showcase language learning. Following this format, they can represent

1. knowledge of the author and genre
2. a genre of choice
3. visual information to support a selected genre—diagrams, photos, graphs, etc.
4. a decoding word study related to the topic

Components of the Daily Letter

1. Author, Title, Genre
2. Text
3. Graphics (Visuals)
4. Reading Word Study (decoding)
5. Ask Me Prompt
6. Comments/Compliments
7. Writing Word Study (encoding)
8. Poetry, Song or Chant
9. Written Response/Reflection
10. Wild Card: choice component

Components of the Daily Letter

Features: Front of the Daily Letter

1. Author, Title, Genre
2. Text
3. Graphics (Visuals)
4. Reading Word Study (decoding)
5. Ask Me… Prompt

Features: Back of the Daily Letter

6. Comments/Compliments
7. Writing Word Study (encoding)
8. Poetry, Song, or Chant
9. Written Response/Reflection
10. Wild Card choice component

5. a prompt for students to respond orally to the topic
6. compliments and comments
7. an encoding word study related to the topic
8. poetry associated with their topic of choice
9. a prompt for a written response topic for the text
10. a wild card activity—a choice activity to further represent their learning

Story-Sharing Daily Letters

There is such satisfaction in watching developing readers enter a discussion with a group about a shared selection, as they begin to notice how they create meaning, to wrestle with ideas, to prove a point by reading a portion of the text, to ask questions about the comments of group members, to draw inferences from the discussion and the words on the page, and to gain insights from their experience with print. They are constructing meaning together, making sense of their own responses to what they have read and heard, mediated by the ideas and feelings of the group members. Suddenly reading has become an interactive process, a socially constructed learning experience (Booth, 2001).

We create a powerful story-sharing community by crafting/composing a wide variety and number of Daily Letters on stories situated in our lives together as a community of learners. We can make the sharing of the Daily Letter a purposeful language experience for the story-sharing community when we design it expressly for our students, about our students, and with our students.

Through this everyday ritual to share our personal stories, we come to know each other so well that we become more thoughtful, responsive, and cooperative with one another. We learn to care deeply about one another and develop a strong sense of community belonging.

As teachers, we begin this process of becoming writers by modeling the writing of our own Daily Letters. We situate them to welcome our students, to invite parents to our open houses, to share personal stories, to write personal narrative about our friends, feelings, and fears, or to construct autobiographies. We share Daily Letters to communicate the things that need to get done or to monitor the actions of the community, such as class rules and expectations, and procedures for doing things such as gym, library, and parent-helper schedules. We can share field-trip information. We can share great passions and expertise on celebratory Daily Letters. We can communicate information on what we know/wonder/learn. We can make the principal, librarian, or secretary, parents, grandparents, or students the subjects of biographies. We craft some Daily Letters to express our feelings and opinions in personal narrative and poetry, while others can persuade members of the class to read a good book.

TOP TEN

Daily Letter Language Experiences from the Lives of Community Members

1. Stories written about and with our friends or family
2. Stories about immediate events in the story-sharing community
3. Stories we have told before or heard before
4. Stories from our imaginations, dreams, and nightmares
5. Stories from other times, languages, or cultures
6. Stories that teach, explain, or persuade

Sharing important life stories helps class members become comfortable talking, working, and being with one another. Attachments and security will develop as they gain experience and confidence sharing the stories that matter most to them.

7. Stories that frighten us
8. Stories that amuse or comfort us
9. Stories that help us remember or forget
10. Stories that strengthen us

(Adapted from Booth & Barton, 2000)

Jacquie's Daily Letter on Michael is a deeply emotional one for all of us. Her personal narrative is about her brother who passed away after a valiant battle with cancer at the age of fourteen. This Daily Letter facilitates Jacquie's sharing of this important family story. Jacquie decides that her genre will be a celebration of Michael. She writes personal narrative about his medical condition and some expository text about the Relay for Friends, an annual relay run held in Vancouver for families touched by cancer. Rather than supporting her written text with a photograph of Michael, Jacquie chooses to bring a collection of framed pictures to school as part of her Daily Letter sharing.

The Relay For A Friend   Jacquie Genre: personal narrative + expository text

My brothers full name is Michael Buddy Robinson. He was diagnosed with leukemia, which is blood cancer. Michael went to Children's Hospital where Taylor's Mom was his nurse. Michael Cucconie was one of his best friends, he was in the band 2gether.

Michael then went to Canuck Place, which is a place where people go when they know they are going to die. When he passed away he was 14 years old. It was the year 1997.

When Michael went to the Relay For A Friend he raised over 16 thousand dollars for cancer research. This run has been done for ten years to help cancer research. Every year people make teams and run in this twelve hour relay run. This run is on June 2nd, 2001. It takes place in Coquitlam Center. People walk around the track with lit candles at the end of the relay to remember their friends and loved ones who have passed away.

Michael's favourite type of food was Greek food. His favorite sports were baseball and soccer. His favorite ride at Disneyland was the Matterhorn.

1. Michael   2. Canuck Place   3. Jacquie
4. Robinson   5. Mom   6. Friend

We have done the Daily Letter together: ___
Messages: _____

Compliments: _____

Writing Word Study:

Blessed Books:
Author: _____
Illustrator: _____

We will put a team of runners in this relay from Sunshine Hills Elementary. Are you up to the challenge? Parents, we have been given special permission to put a team of runners into the event without an entrance fee. We will also participate for two hours rather than the whole twelve hours. We will just need to bring a lunch and ten dollars if you wish to buy a t-shirt.

Front   *Back*

Do you communicate in a wide variety and number of genres with your students and their parents through letters, notes, phone calls? Including this purposeful information on the Daily Letter lets the students not only learn to read and write from it, but also be informed about their day-to-day plans and learn a host of new genres.

Genre Sharing and Intertextual Learning

We introduce our students to a wide variety and number of authors, illustrators, and genres with the sharing of each new Daily Letter. The members of the class take turns sharing situations, reminders, learning, reflections, discussions, problem solving, plans, or invitations. They also have the choice to present a number of more traditional literary genres, such as fairy tales and tall tales, or their own personal narrative, description, or expository text. We can use the Daily Letter as

11

a flexible format to share a wide variety and number of genres, that teach a diverse variety of functions of language. We can make analogies between various genres as we learn more and more of them.

The students are thrilled to be going on a field trip in the third week of school. It is early September and I know that the Burnaby Village Museum will not yet be busy with school groups. The students remind me that they really like going on field trips, and are very excited. I am excited to begin the process of cultivating the idea of how good writers discover their subject through what they notice on this simulated trip back in time to Burnaby, B.C., in 1921.

I use one Daily Letter to communicate the information about the field trip: the date, time, clothing, and lunch requirements for the students and parents. Another Daily Letter will make a request for parent helpers to go on the trip and help with classroom activities when we return. The students read a Daily Letter that I have created about the one-room school they will spend the morning. I use the brochures I have received from the museum and the teacher's notes to cut and paste an informative Daily Letter for the students. Another Daily Letter compares the life of a student in the Seaforth One-Room School of 1921 to the life of a student in a public school in 2003. When we return from the trip, the students use Daily Letters to publish their stories on their adventures in the one-room school. One more Daily Letter thanks the parents and students for their participation in the field trip. Much of my communications with families regarding the field trip are part of the Daily Letter literacy learning each day of their children.

Daily Letter by By Angela - - Genre: Expository text

Burnaby Village

I'm going to tell you about the parker 119 Carousel and all the happiene it brings to people!

The Parker 119 Carousel was built in 1912! The carousel number is 119, because it was the one hundred nineteeth carousel to be made. The number 119 Carousel originaly came from Kanses,where The Wizard Of Oz was made!

There are four art forms used in the making of the carousel. First all the body parts on the hores are hand carved, including the panels and the floor. There are lots more to a carousel than the art, there's machinery, the most important part of the carousel, because it's what makes it all go! The painting of a horse takes 20 hours and 20 people to make a horse, one hour per person. There's about 10-16 coats of paint on each horse! Did you now that on the whole carousel there are 848 lights altogether!

On the Parker 119 Carousel there are 36 horses and they each way 100lbs, altogether the horses would way 3600 pounds!

Mostly all the cantels on the horses are different, like corn cobs, fish, dogs cats, roses, foxes, flags, birds and Indians.

Some horses names are Champion, Old Paint, Scampering Dawn,Treasur,Tommy.D, Vanessa, Vivian, Far Lap, Mr.Edd, James, Fire and Barnaby!

Scampering Dawn is my favorite, most beautiful hores that I ever saw on the carousel. She stood out like a shiny jewell She had lots of pink flowers with red jewels inside of them, her saddle was lined with gold ribbon and two little bows tied on each side. Down below her saddle she had three different types of flowers with blue jewels inside them, and her whole body was all white, I think scampering dawn is the prettiest hores on the Parker 119 Carousel!

Tom Irvine's house was built in 1911, and he lived in it till 1958! He died when he was 100 years old! Tom Irvine was a bachelor, that means he had no wife and no children! Tom Irvine had a really small house, it only had two rooms, no electricity no running water and barely any kitchen. Tom's work was building railroads.

1Burnaby 2Village 3-119
4Parker 5Carousel 6old

Front

---

we have done the Daily Letter together. __
Messages:_____

Compliments: _____

_____ The Batemans house is huge, it was built in 1922. Mr. and Mrs.
_____ Bateman were one of the family's that had a gramma phone. Their
- - - - - - - - - parlour was big! Mary was the mother and Edwin was the father ,May
_____ and Warren were their children. Though the batemans had a big house
_____ their kitchen was pretty small! In their kitchen they have an ice box,
- - - - - - - - - that you would wait for an ice man to bring you a big block of ice to
_____ keep food cold like a fridg. In the batemans house they had a special
_____ rule , and it was called "Ladies First !"
- - - - - - - - -
_____ Jessie and Martha Love's farmhouse is pretty big, it's light yellow
_____ and a shade of dark brown. Jessie and Martha farm for a living. They
- - - - - - - - - had eleven hildren together! They had so many children that they had to
_____ keep building on to their house. Their kitchen was so big that they
_____ decided to move their bathroom in the kitchen so that the hot water
- - - - - - - - - wouldn'd have to travel so far! Jessie and Marthas ceiling in their
_____ parlour was made out of tin!
- - - - - - - - -
_____ Mr. and Mrs. Bell owned the store called Bells Dry Goods, they
_____ lived in the back of the store! Mrs. Bell ran the cash register. Mr. Bells
_____ name is William, and Mrs. Bells name is Flora. At Bells Dry Goods they
- - - - - - - - - sold things like hats, buttens, thread, dolls, baby clothes, girls clothes,
_____ boys clothes but they mostly sold matereal for people to make their own
_____ style of clothes!
- - - - - - - - -

Retelling, Relating, Reflect

- - - - - - - - -
_____   (photo of
- - - - - - - - -   Parker 119
_____   Carousel)
- - - -
- - - - - - - - -

Back

12

On the day after our field trip, some of the students choose to retell their experience in the Seaforth School, and others write about some of the homes they visit in the village museum. Some of them write about their ride on Parker 119, the restored turn-of-the-century carousel. It is exciting for these students as writers to connect with my talk-aloud of how good writers notice things from their own experiences such as these. They are all keen to write Daily Letters about their own special noticings to share with the rest of the class and their families.

The field trip to Burnaby Village is great for community-building through situated, social, and active writing. The students are keen, and so are their parents in this third week of school. The Daily Letters serve to bind the fledgling community of learners together to begin our exploration of a variety of language experiences and genres.

As a Teacher-Led Literacy Event

The Daily Letter can be conceptualized as a literacy event to share a language experience with our students. We can take a half-hour (Grade 1) to an hour (Grade 7) each day to nurture these collaborative literacy-learning events. The Daily Letter becomes the predictable, daily, one-hour class routine for our community to share our important stories. (See BLM #2 page 14.)

On our first day together as a Grade 3 class, I share a Welcoming Daily Letter. I have carefully crafted this Daily Letter, making sure I have written a text that includes the names of every student in the class on it. I introduce myself as the author, and introduce the genre and title. We choral read the text together. Everyone tracks along on their own copy. Two volunteers track it on the overhead as we read.

I prompt some talk about the text by asking the students to find a letter, word, phrase, or sentence on the Daily Letter page that is important to them, and ask them to highlight it with their new neon highlighters. I encourage them to share the word that they have selected and coded with the rest of the class. Hands shoot up as students volunteer to talk.

"I pick *Steven*!" Steven grins as he responds.

"Why did you pick the word *Steven*, Steven?"

"I picked *Steven* because it is my name! Without it you couldn't call me."

The students giggle. Some of them are watching me to see what my reaction is. I smile back and press for more words from Steven. I restate what Steven has said to the rest of the class.

"Steven is saying his name is important. Does anyone have anything to add to this?"

"I do . . . Steven is my friend, we play soccer together."

Already, I have begun the process of encouraging the students to do the talking. I wait patiently for each student's response. I listen carefully to the students, and encourage the other students to give them many opportunities to share their thinking.

"Could you all please find the word *Steven* on your Daily Letter page and highlight it? Get help from your neighbor if you cannot find the word on the page, or look at the overhead to see it being highlighted there."

I also remind the students to have a reason why they have selected the letter, word, etc., and to share this with us. A lively conversation about the text continues.

"I pick *Michelle*, for she is my friend since we were little." Jacquie smiles as we highlight the word *Michelle*.

Michelle responds," I pick *Jacquie* for she is my friend."

Jackie pipes up, "Everyone spells my name wrong." She explains how the name Jacquie can be spelled several different ways.

Routine of the Daily Letter

1. Introduce the author to the class ➪ several minutes
   Introduce the title to the class ➪ one minute
   Introduce genre to the class, make analogies between genres ➪ 3 minutes

2. Work with the text (Title) ➪ 20 minutes
   a. Use a pre-reading strategy
   b. Read the text, talk about it, code/highlight it together

3. Talk about the graphics ➪ several minutes

4. Reading Word Study: select several students to read (decode) 6–8 words ➪ one minute

5. Ask Me…: select students to answer this prompt ➪ 2–3 minutes

6. Comments and/or Compliments

7. Writing Word Study: students write (encode) 6–8 words on their DL ➪ 12 min.

8. Read and talk about the poetry, chant, or song ➪ 10 minutes

9. Students write a response ➪ 10 minutes

10. Wild Card: share choice activity on their Daily Letter ➪ ? Minutes

As the students continue to talk about the text, I scan the room to confirm that all the students are engaged in our first social and active shared-reading experience of the Daily Letter.

In our first shared literacy event we have explored making personal connections to our own names through talking and coding/highlighting the important text. Although I have not chosen to work with each component of the Daily Letter yet, it is a start. Soon we will be able to talk about all of the components of the Daily Letter within a half-hour. We are on our way to learning all about ourselves. We are on our way to learning about each other. We are on our way to learning how to collaborate and to talk about the text to learn more about it.

This is a rich data-gathering opportunity for me as a teacher. I learn many things about the interests, needs, and abilities of my students. I listen carefully, for they have much to say! I watch carefully, for they have much to share.

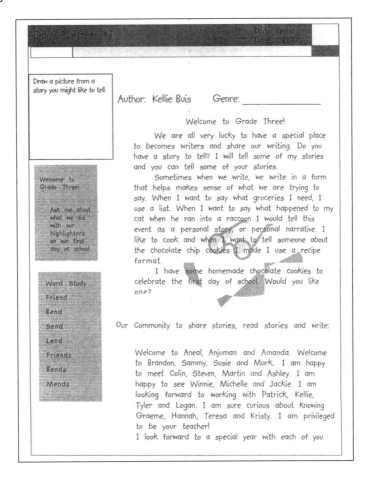

TOP TEN

Ways to Win Your Students' Hearts and Get Inside Their Heads

1. create an active, situated, social way to live together
2. talk together every day about your life together
3. create together every day
4. dramatize together—play together
5. read, write, eat, laugh, draw together
6. share your self as a complete person (including opinions, emotions, successes, failures, dreams, hopes, laughs); be a real person in front of them

7. create, share Daily Letters together
8. honor the knowledge and experiences of the students
9. appeal to your students' need for survival, love, belonging, power, freedom, fun
10. connect the material they read/write to them, to their worlds, and to their cultures

Strategic Approach to Literacy Learning

We create a powerful story-sharing community by engaging our students in a variety and number of think-aloud strategies with the Daily Letter. Our students are introduced to an author's explicit sharing of a think-aloud strategy to go with each of the ten components of the Daily Letter. Through the shared language literacy event, the story-sharing community is introduced to active whole-group strategic talk about the Daily Letter itself and the author's acts of writing and/or reading of each part of it.

Children begin to understand who they are as literacy learners with each Daily Letter literacy event. They grow to understand what it means to learn. To do this they need to talk about how they go about planning, monitoring, and revising their own thinking as readers and writers. They have to be able to reflect on how they determine, for themselves, if they understand how they learn to read and write.

The Daily Letter think-alouds familiarize students with many of the strategies that readers and writers use. Modeling think-aloud strategies each day makes visible the invisible, the in-the-head thinking processes that good readers and writers use. They foster in the students an awareness of the qualities of effective reading and writing.

There are a number of think-aloud strategies our story-sharing community can use to become more strategic, sophisticated, and independent readers, writers, speakers, and listeners. See BLM #3 on page 17 for some of the think-aloud strategies we teach our students during the Daily Letter.

As a Student-Led Literacy Event

As our students accumulate a wealth of knowledge and skills about reading, writing, listening, and speaking, they move out of the role of participating as students in the teacher's sharing of a Daily Letter, into the role of composing their own and sharing them with the larger story-sharing community. We use student-led literacy learning events as a social, collaborative, active method to empower our students to become self-directed leaders of their very own shared language experience.

Active Learning

The students are active in their writing and presenting of Daily Letters in the sense that they learn by talking and doing the Daily Letter. Bruner reminds us that writing in genres is active when, for example, narrative is an instrument for meaning-making and requires work on the writers part, "reading it, making it, analyzing it, understanding its craft, seeing its uses, discussing it" (1996, page 41).

Strategies of the Daily Letter

Strategies Used With Components on the Front of the Daily Letter

1. Author, Title, Genre Component
   - Author Share
   - Analogies Between Texts

2. Text Component
   - Activating Prior Knowledge
   - Pupil Partner Read
   - Radio Read
   - Silent Support
   - Coding the Text
   - Building the Word Wall

3. Graphics Component
   - Visualization
   - Visual Artist Share

4. Reading/Decoding Word Study Component
   - "Say It Fast!"

5. Ask Me… Component
   - 30-Second Talk

Strategies Used With Components on the Back of the Daily Letter

6. Comments/Compliment Component
   - Three Stars and a Wish

7. Writing/Encoding Word Study
   - See It, Say It, Check It

8. Poetry, Song, or Chant Component
   - Poet Share
   - Choral Reading of the Poetry

9. Written Response/Reflection Component
   - Recall, Relate, and Reflect

10. Wild Card Component
    - Think Aloud

We empower our students to compose and share their own Daily Letters, and challenge them to actively become stronger readers, writers, listeners, speakers, and thinkers. They work hard with the Daily Letter format: planning it, composing it, reading it, analyzing it, understanding its craft, seeing its uses; teaching it, discussing it, and sharing it at school and in the home. Rogoff reminds us that cognitive development of an individual occurs in contexts where "children are active in learning and in managing their social partners, and their partners are active in structuring situations that provide children with access to observe and participate in culturally valued skills and perspectives" (Rogoff, 1990, p. 37).

The creating of Daily Letters is highly engaging for Steven, a student who loves to speak, write, and represent with others. He thrives with the opportunity to work with a partner or in a small group to compose a variety and number of genres for the Daily Letter. He makes a Wayne Gretzky Daily Letter with one of the hockey players in the class as a part of our study on Canada. He writes a travel journal on his trip to the Badlands of Alberta with a classmate who is from Alberta. He partners with Kelvin, another friend, to produce an origami Daily Letter. He and his walking field-trip partner write a summary of their visit to the blacksmith shop in Burnaby Village Museum.

Overall, Steven produces about 20 Daily Letters over the course of the year, most of them composed with a variety of friends. Steven and his partners like to lead the sharing of their Daily Letters together. Steven is a natural leader, confident to guide the whole class to listen, read, and view several of his Daily Letters each month. With 22 students in the class, he has several chances to share a Daily Letter each month.

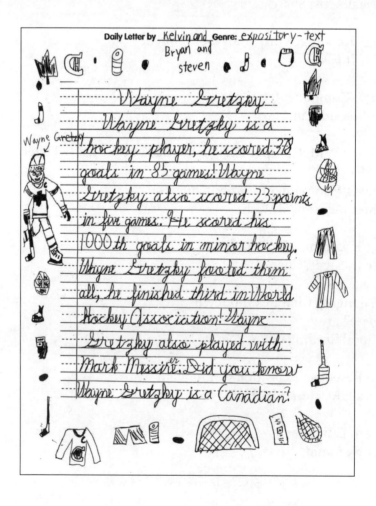

Steven improves his leadership and presentation skills each time he guides the whole class through the active examination of each of the components of his Daily Letter. He especially likes having the students use the think-aloud strategy to code the text with highlighter and talk about their understanding of the text. He walks around, checking how the students are marking their copies of the Daily Letter, as his partner remains standing at the front of the class. He selects a prompt to guide everyones' sharing in the talk about text of the Daily Letter. Steven is a situated, social, and active writer who does an excellent job of taking full responsibility for his self-directed learning and the learning of the other students.

Social Learning

This shared literacy event is also social in the sense that the sharing is done inclusively, with each member of the class participating. The Daily Letter emphasizes a daily routine for purposeful, social, and collaborative strategic communication within the community of learners.

More than 30 years ago, educator James Moffat posited the need to make the solitary acts of reading and writing socially constructed events if we want to promote literacy. Moffat reminded us then, and David Booth reminds us now, that students may be our greatest classroom asset (2001).

TOP TEN

Ways to Make the Daily Letter Social

1. shared reading of several read-alouds each day
2. shared reading of a Daily Letter text and poetry each day
3. shared crafting of Daily Letters in partners or small groups
4. peer proofread and edit of Daily Letters
5. shared practice of Daily Letter presentations in partners or small groups
6. assisting each other during the Daily Letter sharing
7. shared writing of compliments and comments on the Daily Letter
8. shared reading of each other's responses
9. shared writing of word study on the back of the Daily Letter
10. guided reading of the Daily Letter in small groups during centres

Angela stands tall with pride as she waits at the front of the class with her Daily Letter—Ghostylox and the Three Vampires—in hand. The students, sitting in cozy groups of four, organize their highlighters, pencils, and copies of her Daily Letter on their desks. Two students stand ready at the overhead projector. They are set to track Angela's story on the overhead transparency. The rest of the students are busy previewing their own copies of the student-authored story. It is October, and Angela is the first student in the Grade 3 class to share a Daily Letter.

Author, Title, Genre

Angela waits to see that her peers are listening and ready to track the story. She begins by introducing herself. "Welcome to my Daily Letter. I am an author of a Halloween fairy tale Ghostylox and the Three Vampires. I got my ideas from 'The 13 Nights of Halloween.' I adapted the fairy tale *Goldilocks and the Three Bears* to Ghostylox and the Three Vampires. Writers get their ideas from other books they have read."

Before Angela begins reading, I record Angela's strategy of how good writers get their ideas from other stories and authors on the What Good Writers Do chart as the students watch.

What Good Writers Do

Good writers research their topic.
Good writers have a good lead sentence.
Good writers begin with action.
Good writers make pictures in your mind.
Good writers show, not tell.
Good writers choose their words carefully.
Good writers choose their characters' names carefully.
Good writers make their title last, sometimes
Good writers search for specifics.
Good writers notice things in their everyday life.
Good writers get their ideas from books.

As I move to the back of the class so Angela can begin her sharing, I reflect on the effort Angela has put into creating this Daily Letter. I remember how excited she was when she got the idea for her Halloween fairy tale from several read-alouds we had shared together. Angela especially liked "The 13 Nights of Halloween," adapted by Rebecca Dickinson from the Christmas carol "The Twelve Days of Christmas." I beam with pride when I think of what a confident author Angela has become. I also marvel at Angela's readiness to be the first student to lead the sharing of her own Daily Letter with the class.

HAPPY HALLOWEEN!

Once along time ago, there was three vampires. There was GREAT BIG sized papa vampire, a medium sized mama vampire, and a teensy weensy baby vampire. When they went out to scare all the children on a cold halloween night they accidently left there door open and a little ghost named Ghostylox flew in the haunted house that belonged to the three vampires. When she got in it there were three bowls of bat soup with green slime on them. Ghostylox said" yum !, how can these things leave this stuff out." She tasted a little bit out of each bowl she liked the last bowl the best so she ate it all up.Ghostylox felt tired so she flew to the coffins. She sat in the first coffin and the lid was to heavy to lift up so she flew to the next coffin and she said, "the lid is still to heavy to lift up", so she flew to the last coffin and she said "this one is just right", and it was so comfortable that she fell a sleep in it. After hours the vampires came home to there house from scaring all the children on halloween night.When they came in they saw that someone had been tasting their bat soup. Papa vampire said," someones been tasting my bat soup !" in a mad voice.Then mama vampire said," someones been tasting my bat soup and it's almost gone." Then baby ampire said," someones been tasting my bat soup and it's all gone !" The three vampires were so tired so they went upstairs to go to bed. But when they got there they saw that someone had been sleeping in there coffins. Papa vampire said," someones been sleeping in my coffin," said papa in a mad voice. Then mama vampire said," someones been sleeping my coffin and made it all messy." Then baby vampire said, " someones been sleeping in my coffin and there it is !" Ghostylox heard the vampires and got scared so she flew out of the open window in the room. The End.

GHOSTYLOX AND THE THREE VAMPIRES by Angela

Front

We have done the Daily Letter together: ___
Messages:_____
_____
Compliments: _____
_____

Writing Word Study:

Blessed Books:
Author: _____
Illustrator:_____

Poems, Songs and Chants

My Halloween Time Line

1996 : I was a Pnik princess
1997 : I was a ninga
1998 : I was a whtie and gold angel
1999 : I was a black cat
2000 : I am going to be a witch   by Angela

HALLOWEEN

On halloween all the scary ones come out like !
Vamipres who go scaring little children,
Ghost who go giving a booooo !
Scelatins who hang in hallways or doors,
And wolfs who try to bite you.
by Angela

Back

Pre-reading Strategy, Reading, Coding the Text

For her pre-reading strategy, Angela asks the students to notice that her Daily Letter connects to Goldilocks and the Three Bears. She asks the students to share what they already know about this fairy tale for several minutes.

After Angela finishes listening to the students share their prior knowledge of the fairy tale, she asks the students to look for parts of her scary tale that are similar to other fairy tales, and then begins to read her Daily Letter out loud. Her voice booms for "GREAT BIG sized papa vampire," softens for "a medium sized mama vampire," and plunges to a pale, trembling "and a teensy, weensy baby vampire." Angela's stellar use of her voice has all the students flailing their arms to be chosen to read it too. Angela selects Mary to reread it. The other students track the story with their fingers as she reads. Angela thanks Mary for using a wonderful papa, momma, and baby voice for her read-aloud.

Next everyone uncaps their highlighters and prepares to study the text. Angela glances to the nearby wall to a large chart that she has displayed within easy view of her audience. She has chosen to approach her talk about text from the stance of a reader making a personal response to it and will use a list of prompts to help her guide the students' talk about her text.

Angela reads from the chart: "Please find a word, phrase, or sentence on the Daily Letter that connects to your life."

Steven responds, "I pick *haunted house*. I have been in a haunted house. I got into an old house and I wasn't scared."

Angela invites all the students to find *haunted house* on their own pages and highlight it. The two students by the overhead projector underline each word or phrase on the transparent copy of Angela's story as it is discussed. She thanks Steven and selects another student to respond.

"I pick the word *trembling*. I have been in a very old house and I was so scared. I was trembling so much!" responds Mary.

The students highlight the word *trembling* on the page.

"Mrs. Buis, can you add the word *trembling* to the -*ing* column on the Word Wall?" Angela requests. I respond by adding the word in orange, the color I will use for each new word that we add from a Daily Letter in October. I will list the November words in red. I am hoping that using different colors will help students find any special words they are looking for during independent writing times.

Angela selects several other prompts, such as favorite words and least favorite words. She glances at the overhead from time to time to see if the two students working there have continued to highlight the words as well. She glances at Annie, who is busy looking at the overhead to help her locate the word on her own page.

I pad softly around the room, supporting students or whispering specific, sincere compliments to them regarding their effort on this Daily Letter. Students whisper quietly around the room in response to the conversation Angela leads. Some students assist their neighbors with their search through the text for words. I add each word to the word wall as it is discussed.

Angela continues to conduct her sharing of the text for about 20 minutes. Engagement of the students is high.

Word Studies

When Angela is finished sharing the text component of the Daily Letter, she goes on to have the students read the word list below her story. She talks about the strategies she uses to read these words. She asks the students to talk about the patterns they see in the list. Several students volunteer to explain the pattern—and the exceptions to the pattern—in *hour*, *sour*, *power*, *tower*, *flower*, *soup*, *coup*, *troop*, *loop*. The students agree that English is an interesting language.

Back of the Daily Letter

Once Angela has shared the components on the front of the Daily Letter, she goes on to proudly share her Halloween poetry on the back. She chooses to number the students and have each group share a line of her poem. She also shares the act of writing the poem, of how her poem came out of her own Halloween experiences.

Angela then engages the students in the written word study. She has a set of eight words carefully selected from her story that follow a pattern: *vampire*, *tire*, *fire*, *hire*, *liar*, *mire*, *wire*, and *choir*. She dictates the first word, and the students print the word on the lines on the back of the Daily Letter. She puts the first word on the board for the students to look at, say, study, and write. The students who were working on the overhead projector are now circulating around the room to check how the students are doing at encoding the words. We are especially careful to check how the students have printed the words *liar* and *choir*. The students check their own writing of the words as well.

Concluding the Daily Letter Sharing

Angela completes her Daily Letter by giving the students some time to respond to her story in writing on the lines at the bottom of the Daily Letter page. "Can you relate to the part of my fairy tale you liked?"

Angela and her two assistants cruise around the room sharing in on the responses that the students are busy writing. At the end of the hour-long sharing of the Daily Letter, the students break into a spontaneous round of applause for Angela.

The composing and sharing cycle of the Daily Letter is complete for Angela except for the home sharing that will take place for each student that night. The challenge for the students to compose and share their stories on the Daily Letter has begun with Angela, an impressive young author.

As a Multi-purpose Teaching Tool

The Daily Letter can be conceptualized as a multi-purpose teaching tool we can use to nurture

- personal power
- community belonging
- critical literacy
- communication skills and strategies
- intertextual learning, the dissolution of curricular boundaries
- unending sources of engaging reading materials/resources
- a strong home–school connection
- an inclusive classroom for at-risk, low-progress students
- an inclusive classroom for ESL students
- a three-dimensional learning model—learning literacy, about literacy, and through literacy

Three-Dimensional Learning with the Daily Letter

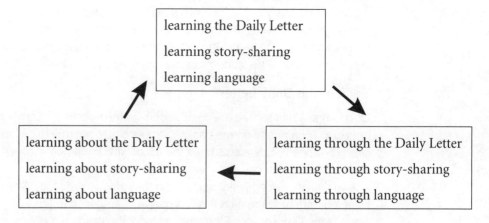

(adapted from Chapman, 1999; Halliday, 1975, 1985)

The knowledge, skill, attitudes, and conceptual development of the entire story-sharing community are nurtured with the sharing of a different student's Daily Letter each day. Our apprentice literacy learners become deeply involved in prolific, purposeful reading, writing, and meaning-making through the crafting of their Daily Letters. They also become immersed in fertile, authentic listening and speaking about the strategies of good readers and writers through the leading of the collaborative talk about the text. Empowered, self-directed literacy learning is cultivated within this strong story-sharing community.

CHAPTER 2

The Daily Language Experience

We prepare Daily Letter sharing as a ritual for our students to develop a variety of communication skills. We plan to have our students engaged for a half-hour to an hour in collaborative story sharing. We plan to have them participate in active learning. We want to be sure to create an inclusive classroom for at-risk, learning-disabled, ESL, and low-progress students by including the support staff in the classroom. We need to ensure that they are organized to work within the classroom at all times. We want to arrange for the Daily Letter routine to be predictable in time, routine, materials, and setting. We want to create a routine for informal assessment during the school day that covers each of the components of a comprehensive literacy learning environment.

When the students arrive, involve them in the Daily Letter as a flexible, open-ended activity that invites them to create multiple modes of representations of their own learning. Invite the students to have a voice in their school life. With these conditions in place, you are on your way to creating an engaging, exciting story-sharing community that matters to students, parents, and yourself.

Format and Routine

We invite our students to participate with oral, written, and visual modes of communication through a two-step Daily Letter process. This involves the teacher or a student writing a genre of their choice and putting this genre into the Daily Letter format, and then following a specific routine to share this format.

Format

First we format our Daily Letter pages to study many of the components of language learning: genre studies, text studies, author studies, graphics, decoding and encoding vocabulary studies, reader responses, and representing of understandings in a variety of modes. See BLMs #4 page 26 and #4A page 27 for the format of the Daily Letter.

Routine

We also use the Daily Letter as our set routine for students to practise the components of a comprehensive language experience. See BLMs #5 page 28 and #5A page 29 to see how the form of the Daily Letter shapes the routine.

K to early Primary: 15–20 minutes
Late Primary 40–60 minutes
Intermediate 60–70 minutes

Day after day, week after week, month after month, the students will become adept at participating in the rigorous daily routine to lead talks about being an author, talks about their text and the vocabulary and graphics that support it. They will become skilled at talking about their poetry, and at retelling, relating, and reflecting on what they have learned. The text, poem, graphics, and word studies work together to provide a rich environment for authentic language development.

A Comprehensive Literacy Program

This format and routine of the Daily Letter takes into account many of our language arts curriculum goals, as well as the needs of individual students, their families, and the community as a whole. We can conveniently use the Daily Letter as a single instructional tool to teach many of the components of a comprehensive literacy program in a short amount of time each day. This routine includes shared/guided reading, shared/guided writing, vocabulary studies, strategies for working with text, poetry, and reader response experiences each day.

See BLMs #6 page 30 and #6A page 31 to see how the Daily Letter shares with a comprehensive literacy learning program the following features that allow for maximum literacy growth of the students (Booth, 2001):

- author, genre, and intertextual study
- shared reading/writing
- guided reading/writing
- curriculum-connected reading and writing
- strategies of visual literacy
- multiple modes of representing learning
- building word power through decoding
- oral and written communication
- building word power through encoding
- genres: chants, poetry, song
- reader response: literature groups and book talk
- assessment and evaluation of all these aspects of literacy learning

---

The Daily Letter is our everyday story-sharing, caring language experience. It gives all my students an invitation to have their voices heard. It is uniquely designed for students like Mary (a middle-of-the-road student), Annie (an at-risk student), and Angela (an exceptional student) to share the responsibility for the literacy learning of the class with me. Not only will they each learn from the process-oriented designing of their Daily Letters, they will also learn from the sharing of their Daily Letter with the discourse community.

Mary, Annie, Angela, and the other fledgling literacy learners will spend from several weeks to several months observing me as I model the sharing of my Daily Letter stories. This prepares them to learn how to effectively lead their own Daily Letter literacy event. When I feel they are ready, I will invite one student to share/instruct her or his own Daily Letter language experience with the class (as Angela did). Over time, I will empower other students to lead their own shared literacy event with their own individually crafted Daily Letter as well.

It will take time to establish the routines of sharing each component of the Daily Letter. It may take you several weeks to a month to explain, model, and guide the practice of the story-sharing community before it goes smoothly.

Daily Letter Format: Front

1. Author: _____   Genre:_____

   Title: _____

2. Text

                                                        3. Graphics

4. Reading Word Study

_____   _____   _____   _____

5. Ask Me what I learned about…

Daily Letter Format: Back

We/I have reviewed the Daily Letter: _____ (initials)

6. Comments: _____

_____

_____

7. Writing Word   8. Poetry, Chants, Songs

    1. _____

    2. _____

    3. _____

    4. _____

    5. _____

    6. _____

    7. _____

    8. _____

9. Written Response _____

_____

_____

_____

10. Wild Card ???

Routine for the Daily Letter: Front

1. Author: _____   Genre:_____

   Introduce the author and the genre to the class.   **Review the genre and qualities of it related to other Daily Letters.**

   Title: _____

2. Text

   Share text by reading it to the class and having everyone read it out loud in unison, in partners, or by themselves. Lead the talk about the text and highlight or code the text with prompts.

3. Graphics

   Talk about how to read graphics. Read them.

4. Reading Word Study

   Talk about strategies to read words. Have students read them.

5. Ask Me what I learned about…

   Respond

Routine for the Daily Letter: Back

We/I have reviewed the Daily Letter: _____ (initials)

6. Comments: _____

   _____

   Student, parent, or teacher can fill this in.

7. Writing Word

   **Dictate 6-8 words from story
   to the students.
   Add them to the Word Wall.**

8. Poetry, Chants, Songs

   **Read the poem, talk about it, and
   maybe illustrate or code it.**

9. Written Response _____

   _____

   _____

   _____

   **Ask the students to respond to the text by retelling, relating, or reflecting on it in
   writing.**

10. Wild Card ???

Features of a Comprehensive Literacy Learning Program on the Daily Letter: Front

1. Author: _____   Genre:_____

   Author Study   **Genre Study**

   Title: _____

2. Text

   Shared/ Guided Reading
   Curriculum-connected Reading and Writing

3. Graphics

   Strategies of Visual Literacy

4. Reading Word Study

   Decoding of Vocabulary taken from text

5. Ask Me what I learned about…

   Oral Communication
   Speaking/Listening

Features of a Comprehensive Literacy Learning Program
on the Daily Letter: Back

We/I have reviewed the Daily Letter: _____ (initials)

6. Comments: _____

_____

Oral/Written Communication

7. Writing Word

   Encoding

8. Poetry, Chants, Songs

   Genres
   Shared Reading
   Guided Reading

9. Written Response _____

_____

_____

_____

Reader Response
Assessment and Evaluation of Written Response

10. Wild Card ???

   Multiple Modes of Representing

Each student has the challenge to craft and share a Daily Letter. This is our everyday ritual to authentically extend our knowledge, skills, abilities, and experiences beyond ourselves. We see our very own interests in print on our Daily Letters. We listen and talk with each other about our special ideas and words.

A different member of the class leads the sharing of the Daily Letter each day. Each student has a turn one or two times each month. I assist the students-as-leaders as they oversee the sharing of their Daily Letter with their peers for the first time. I share my delight as the students talk aloud about the reading and writing they are doing with the other readers and writers in the story-sharing community.

In due course my students grow in their independence of instruction, a process called "transformation of participation" (Rogoff et al, 1996). This sharing of the power, between the students and the text and me, makes us all co-participants in the learning that will take place throughout the year.

Mary, Annie, and Angela are each transformed by their increased participation as apprentices and mentors. Already, I am beginning to notice that the students are becoming independent strategic thinkers. They are becoming more confident with each shift in our roles.

Mary, Annie, and Angela have adopted the belief that they are not solely dependent on teacher direction and me. They have become empowered, critical, self-directed literacy learners and leaders. The Daily Letter becomes a purposeful and meaningful method for my students to share the huge responsibility with me for their learning about literacy, themselves, each other, and the world.

Word Study

Students are empowered to deepen their understanding of words by teaching Daily Letter word studies to the class as part of their Daily Letter sharing. We select words from the text of our Daily Letter and create three word studies to go with it. You will likely need to conference with students during centres/workshop to help them prepare the strategies that they will teach to the class through their Daily Letter.

I communicate the idea that making errors is a natural part of the learning process. This relaxes students to experiment and take risks with language. Each student is encouraged to participate as a problem solver rather than just an information receiver.

Our main goals for the three kinds of word study —decoding words in context, decoding words in isolation, and encoding words—are to be aware of words, to be interested in words, and to be given routine opportunities to increase the number of automatically read/spelled words. The Daily Letter is useful to cover lots of rich vocabulary development.

Vocabulary is essential to reading comprehension, so it is important that we model for our students the many ways to work with it on the Daily Letter. Over time, the students will come to understand numerous ways to decode and encode words. Because our teaching time is limited, however, we need to focus on exactly the words that our students need to know. These words are best learned in the context of the Daily Letter.

We create a powerful story-sharing community by routinely demonstrating to our students the strategies to work with vocabulary. A human mind is designed to try to figure things out, to categorize things and make sense of things. Young students need time to play with words in both oral and written form. The Daily Letter is designed to give students opportunities to play with words in the text, and in isolation from the text. Marilyn Chapman reminds us that "play is the hallmark of intellectual life; playing with words and ideas is the essence of writing" (1997, p. 62).

We expose our students to three word studies each day. We want to have them code the text of the Daily Letter (see Component #2). We want them to work with words in context, but we also want them to encode words taken from the Daily Letter and dictated to the students in isolation from the text (see Component #7).

Components of the Daily Letter Routine

See BLMs #6 page 30 and #6A page 31 to see how the routine follows the components that make up the Daily Letter itself.

Component	Routine
1. Author, Title, Genre	Introduction
2. Text	Shared Reading
	Pre-reading
	Reading
	Talk about the text
3. Graphics	Talk about the graphics
4. Reading Word Study	Decode 6–8 words
5. Ask Me Prompt	Respond orally to the prompt
6. Comments/Compliments	Write comments, compliments
7. Writing Word Study	Encode 6–8 words
8. Poetry, Song or Chant	Read and talk about the poem, song, chant
9. Written Response/Reflection	Write a response/reflection
10. Wild Card: choice component	Depends on the nature of the component

1. Introduction

Literacy specialist Marie Clay (1993) notes "the introduction should be viewed as a time when the teacher prepares the reader to enter into a conversation with the author of the text." The first routine of the Daily Letter is for us to take a few minutes to introduce the students to the author, title, and genre before we begin the shared reading of it. We want to "walk" the students through the text by looking briefly at the title and the text, discussing any special aspects of the letter-size page. We want to give a brief summary of the Daily Letter in two or three statements.

The purpose of this quick summary is to activate students' background knowledge and set them on a semantic or meaning-based cueing system. We can establish the purpose for reading the text with the audience—what's in it for them—and establish how we will read it. We decide together whether we are reading for enjoyment or skimming for information. We want to briefly implant a text outline and draw attention to unique vocabulary or any points of interest before we begin the shared reading of the Daily Letter.

2. Reading

The shared reading of the Daily Letter text is the main event of the Daily Letter. This event is based on the model of the bedtime story, or lap reading, where an adult shares a book with a child by reading it aloud and pointing to the words (Holdaway, 1979). The Daily Letter is a modification of this age-old shared-reading practice. Translating the bedtime experience of shared reading with one or two children at home into the classroom setting of more than 20 children requires some adjustment in the sharing method. Each child in the class needs to comfortably see the text being explored.

In a traditional Holdaway shared reading experience, a big book is used so that each child can easily see the text. For the purposes of shared reading with a whole class, each student has his or her own copy of the Daily Letter to interact with. Distributing an individual copy of the text to students ensures that they can actively participate in the sharing of the text. Each student has the benefit of being able to comfortably see the text to actively code and mark it during the Daily Letter sharing.

Oral reading is integral to comprehension and is thus a critical component of successful reading of the Daily Letter. Traditional methods of fluency, practised through unrehearsed oral reading, did not focus on either comprehension or student engagement. Many of us have upsetting memories of oral reading when we were in school. This does not have to be the case with the Daily Letter.

Engaging our students in effective oral fluency practice is part of the Daily Letter sharing each day. We spend time giving explicit instruction that specifically targets fluency to help our students develop independence and understanding in silent reading. Typically students with inadequate fluency are likely to avoid reading because of fear of failure and negative attitudes. "Students who don't get good at reading don't read" (Anderson et al, 1988).

For late-primary students, fluency is critical. Students are generally expected to read independently from this stage on. As the volume and complexity of reading expectations and material expand, a student who has fluency is able to more easily keep up. The Daily Letter provides explicit modeling and guided practice for the group in independent oral and silent reading. Having the group read the Daily Letter text through in unison guarantees success for everyone, with no one humiliated by lack of ability. A child repeatedly hears words and sees the print, making associations between the letters and sounds within the safety of the group.

Authors who lead the Daily Letter need to plan for their explicit modeling of fluent reading. Students get to listen to an expert read (the author who has rehearsed), follow the print (on their own copies of the Daily), and either repeat the text (echo reading) or read along with the expert reader (choral reading). The author and the students learn to monitor their reading and also learn to monitor their fluency. We can use the Daily Letter as a source of reading material for repeated readings, for talk about oral reading, and to demonstrate a student's efforts on a meaningful piece of text. This part of the Daily Letter appeals to students of all reading abilities because they can all be successful with varying amounts of practice.

3. Graphics

Visual literacy is an important part of the Daily Letter. Visuals are integrated into the Daily Letter text by the author to assist in the meaning-making of it. The author adds graphics that may be designed on the computer or by hand. We want our students to produce visual information to connect with their written material, to teach them how to enrich their expression beyond written ideas. Literacy is more than reading and writing stories; literacy includes reading and writing information as well. Similarly, information literacy is more than communicating with just words; many information texts purposely include important visual elements, such as diagrams, graphs, maps, and tables.

We want our students to learn to read for meaning even if they do not see any words. We want them to make the connection that we often gain greater meaning with the integration of verbal and visual information. This effective research strategy is a powerful aid to comprehension of the Daily Letter.

We use the Daily Letter to model for students a variety and number of ways to take written information and recompose into visuals. After we read the Daily Letter with our students we need to take a few moments to view and interpret the accompanying diagram, graph or chart, time line, etc. We want to use each Daily Letter language experience to communicate to our students new ways to make the text more accessible, memorable, concise, and clear with the addition of visual elements.

We also use visuals on the Daily Letter to teach students the many ways there are to read text. They can practise when and how to read, browse, search, scan, skip, and skim. They learn to make sense of the purpose for reading. Students learn to locate specific information through reading part of the text, or by entering the text in the middle, with no obligation to read it all in sequence. They may choose to follow the author's pathway, that is, to read "the whole story"; or they can choose to read the same text selectively choosing their own path (Moline, p. 6).

Another important benefit of visual text is the assistance it gives to at-risk readers, who may not yet be fluent with words, and who need visuals for access to the text. We want to give at-risk students and/or students with English as a second language a routine to feel successful in their meaning-making of the text. Non-mainstream students have the option to write shorter text for their own Daily Letters, and to support it in visual form until assisted-learning support can be implemented.

We use the visual text component of the Daily Letter to help students integrate their learning across the curriculum. Students develop problem-solving skills in the production of the Daily Letter layout. They are challenged to create fully integrated text that highlights social studies, science, art, and mathematics.

Some of your students will be very challenged by the invitation to provide visual elements on their Daily Letter. They will have to think hard to provide information that appears only in drawings and not in words. Others will become fascinated to find ways to create meaning with few or no words. You can expose students daily to how other members of the class present information through writing and visuals.

4. Reading/Decoding Word Study

There are several lines of words below the main text on the front of the Daily Letter. The author of the Daily Letter prints this list of words from the text. The students practise these words and converse with each other on the strategies and skill associated with reading each during the Daily Letter sharing.

Possible Word Studies

This list suggests samples of the kinds of Reading Word Study we can prepare for the front of our Daily Letter:

- Useful Words:
    The, of, and, a, to, in

- Semantic Mapping—similarities/differences between words:
    nature, picture, richer, stitched, switcher
    oppose, opposite, opposition, opposed, opposing

- Spelling Demons (Fry, Kress & Fountoukidis, 2000):
    Wear, weather, weigh, were, we're, when, where, which, white

- Patterned Words, Phonograms (Fry et al, 2000):
    red, bed, fed, led, Ned
    reed, bead, feed, lead, need
    are, arm, army, artist, arctic

- Phonetically Irregular Words (Fry et al, 2000):
    - should, would, could, said, was, once, again, does, your, were, where

- Homophones (Fry et al, 2000)—first word from the Daily Letter:
    - Sea (ocean), see (visualize); seam, seem; serf, surf; sow, so, sew

- Confusing Words (Fry et al, 2000):
    - accede, exceed; accept, except; alley, ally; catch, ketch; angel, angle

- Analyzing roots and affixes (Fry et al, 2000):
    - non- (not): nonsense, nonfiction, nonresistant, nonstop,
    - dia- (through, across): diameter, dialogue, diagonal, diagnose
    - uni- (one): unicorn, uniform, unite, universe, unique, unison
    - -ness (state or quality of): kindness, happiness, goodness, darkness

- Revised Word—easy–difficult words such as synonyms (Fry et al, 2000):
    - Say – remark, seem – appear, mad – crazy, name – title, large – enormous

- Word Origins (Fry et al, 2000):
    - bio (life in Greek): biology, biography, biochemistry, biopsy, biosphere

- Topic or Key Vocabulary:
    - cent, change, coin, cost, dime, dollar, dollar sign, nickel, penny, loonies

- Mnemonic Devices—to remember difficult words:
    - once: only nice cats eat
    - because: big elephants can always use speckled eggs

Do you think your students are capable of instructing their own word study with their Daily Letter? Students can be trained into a leadership role to dictate a list of words and have the rest of the students go through a step-by-step process to see each word on the board, say it, write it, and check it.

5. Ask Me . . . Prompt

One the bottom of the front of the Daily Letter is an "Ask me ...." We provide a sentence stem or prompt for parents or caregivers to engage in a conversation with their child each night. The Ask me... prompt is usually related to the information provided on the Daily Letter, to get more than "Nothing happened at school today" from the student. A specific question can be asked of the child at home through this Daily Letter structure:

Student reads Ask me . . . prompt to the parent: Ask me my favorite part of the book The *Polar Express.*

The parent then restates the prompt to child: What was your favorite part of the book The *Polar Express*?

6. Comments / Compliments

Comments

The communication with parents or caregivers is an important communication genre on the Daily Letter. Students see notes from the teacher to the child and their parents, and notes that come back from the parent and child to the teacher.

There is a place for the parent to sign or initial if they have worked with the Daily Letter with their child that night.

Copies of the Daily Letter are kept in a folder or binder on each student's desk, so children can reread them on their own during free time or planned individual reading time. The binder goes home each night so the child and caregiver can lap read the text. The student returns it to school in the morning with the Daily Letter signed (on the back) as being read by the parent or caregiver and the child. The child may go back and reread old favorites. Parents can review those Daily Letters their child may have had difficulties with.

Compliments

The reward for a job well done on the Daily Letter genre is…a job well done. There is no effort or attention given in the form of rewards, points, coupons, or gold stars. The improvements in reading and writing on the Daily Letter are typical reminders of a growing competency and the fostering of self-efficacy in the literacy learner.

The readers, writers, and presenters of the Daily Letter are given compliments that inform them about the particulars of their job well done. When the student-as-teacher is leading the Daily Letter, the teacher is free to move around the room, complimenting individuals. The students can be complimented on their accomplishments with sincere recognition of the details of their efforts or achievement. The complimenting of a student is typically done quietly to each student as an individual, and indicates the specific aspects of effort or achievement or both. Wlodkowski reminds us that praise should be 3S–3P: "sincere, specific, sufficient and properly given for praiseworthy success in the manner preferred by the learner" (1985; cited in Guthrie & Wigfield, 1997).

7. Writing Word Study

The Writing Word Study is located on the back of the Daily Letter. These lines are for students to write a list of words dictated by the author/leader during their Daily Letter. Not only do students need to solve words in reading (decoding, as they do on the front of the Daily Letter), they need to solve words in writing (encoding, as they do on the back of the Daily Letter). The list of words causes students to relate and reflect upon the words, their spelling and meaning. Writing words actively challenges students to think about print. The more opportunities students have to write, the greater the likelihood that they will reproduce spellings of words they have seen and heard (Clay, 1991). On the Daily Letter, we write the words we have seen and heard in context of the text on the front of the Daily Letter.

Students need lots of practice transposing spoken words into written symbols through dictation. The Writing Word Study is a concrete demonstration of the written word. Shared writing of words can be modeled as a pause before a letter or word is written, followed by saying the word slowly and stretching out the sounds as students write it.

Children must be familiar with the notion that sounds can be put together to form words. This is developmentally easier than the opposite—taking whole words and dividing them apart into their constituent phonemes. Blending can be a strong predictor of reading ability just prior to the beginning of reading instruction and through Grade 1.

Students need lots of feedback and support if they are to be confident, independent readers and writers. It is important to focus on a student's accomplishments, on what they can do. Future successes are built on past successes. It is a responsibility of both the teacher and parents to encourage students in their development as readers and writers.

The Daily Letter event gives students opportunities daily, not weekly as is usually associated with traditional Monday-to-Friday spelling tests, to practise strategies to both read and write words. By placing 8 to 10 words on the front of the Daily Letter to be read, and leaving space to write approximately 8 to 10 words on the back, we support the students' development of self-confidence and the belief that they can be competent readers and writers.

8. Poetry

Donald Graves (1992) reminds us that sharing the sound and sense of a poem can be one of the most delightful moments in the teaching day. This is the favorite component of the Daily Letter for many children in the class.

Poetry is not only a popular aspect of the Daily Letter, it is also a very important aspect of it. David Booth cautions us that "It is important to note that unless teachers read poetry to their students, they are unlikely to experience poetry as an important part of their lives" (1996, p. 80).

On the back of the Daily Letter there is room for a poem, a song, or a chant. It may be a poem the author has found to go with the theme of the Daily Letter, or one the author has written. The author knows when his or her turn is coming up, and can practise with a voice that will capture the spirit of the poem. The sharing of the poem may take a moment, or as long as 20 minutes if there is interest from the community of learners.

We get our students to enter into poetry by setting a purpose or a way to read it. We may want to give a brief summary statement of the poem, as with the genre shared on the front of the Daily Letter. You could begin by making a personal connection such as "I picked this poem because…." There may be special features of the text to draw attention to, or you might just begin to recite the poem without interruption. Try to make sure there is a lot of silence around the first reading (Heard, 1999, p. 31). Some poets may wish to recite their poems from memory. They need to make a confident stance and recite it clearly. We want them to face the audience and used big gestures if the poem lends itself to it, and to take a bow at the end. It is more effective to read the poem through several times.

By the end of the year, each student will have a collection of more than 200 poems, songs, and chants that have been shared daily in the classroom and nightly in the home. By the end of the year a student will moderate more than ten shared poetry readings during their Daily Letter language experience.

Poetry on the Daily Letter is designed to be read aloud. With the Daily Letter, a student learns how to demonstrate the reading of poetry out loud, and develop fluency (which is critical to comprehension). The reading and rereading of poetry through read-aloud and choral reading promote fluency.

Poetry, songs, and chants on the Daily Letter assist students' participation in reading performance. Students learn to read with the rhythmic choral reading. High-achieving students have opportunities to benefit from fluency practice and to make personal decisions about how a character may be portrayed or a poem interpreted.

Choral reading is a fun way for the leader to manipulate the Daily Letter text and be creative about the ways he or she shares and demonstrates it. An apprentice writer learns about the music of language through exposure to the choral reading of rhymes, chants, songs, and poetry. Playing with the sounds of the poems and songs develops phonemic awareness, a powerful predictor of later reading success. Engaging our students in choral reading of rhymes and rhythms allows them to associate the symbols they see on their Daily Letter with the sounds they hear. The spoken word has special power to promote this learning.

9. Written Response

The Daily Letter fosters growth in reading, writing, responding, and reflection for all students. It is a large group opportunity to deepen students' ability to respond

Try nurturing your students' poetry writing as a special way of noticing or sharing something of interest in their life—good times, bad times, and whatever happens between. Try cultivating the idea of poetry as the sharing of the moments we capture, the everyday thoughts, feelings, and experiences we craft into words. Students from a young age can write wonderful poetry when given lots of invitations, time, and encouragement to write from their heart and soul.

personally and share their thinking in a community setting where their opinions and responses are valued.

The space on the back, at the bottom, is where the thinking and learning that has taken place during the Daily Letter event can be retold, related to, and reflected on. This is an opportunity for students to think about their understandings and share them with others.

Researchers have looked at the benefits of having students write in open-ended ways about their thinking. Such purposeful writing is much more meaningful to a student than workbook pages. It is also much more useful from an assessment point of view: a student is representing his or her thinking and may be approximating most of the text. This is an invitation to write without the expectation that the text be perfect or have the "right answer."

This part of the Daily Letter is used to assess the thinking of the students rather than their writing abilities. They can talk about the content of the Letter. Students relate in writing by briefly sharing what they may feel strongly about in relationship to the Daily Letter. Relating is the process of connecting their experiences or feelings about the content of the Daily Letter. Reflecting is the asking of questions that arise out of the Daily Letter event.

Mini-lessons

Each of the parts of the Daily Letter is actually a mini-lesson (vocabulary, text share, poetry, etc.). The space on the bottom of the back of the Daily Letter can be used by the teacher of the Daily Letter for a readers' response, or it can be used as a place to check the understanding of the students. It can also be used as a place to have students respond to a mini-lesson that arises out of confusion over any of the other components of the Daily Letter. A mini-lesson may be based on the needs of the students observed by the teacher during the sharing of the Daily Letter. The space at the bottom of the Daily Letter provides room to demonstrate or teach a specific skill or idea in a short, purposeful way.

A mini-lesson—as a brief, focused teaching of one aspect of the Daily Letter that remains unclear to the majority of the students—can take from several minutes to ten minutes. Mini lessons have a "showing" and not "telling" quality. Students may use the lines on the back of the Daily Letter as a practice ground for a new writing idea, such as a lead for a story, a name for a specific character, or a brief review of how to use a convention of print, such as an exclamation mark or a comma. Some mini-lessons require only conversation on a topic and require no formal written work. A good mini-lesson should be short, specific and relevant.

10. Wild Card—Special Features

The format of the Daily Letter changes with the literacy needs of the students. There are many possibilities of new features or structures to create a genre most suitable to meet the multiple instructional goals of a particular group of children. The Daily Letter is flexible enough to stretch the thinking and understanding each unique community of learners.

Create a predictable daily routine.

Managing Routines

We can create a powerful story-sharing community by setting up a predictable routine for distributing the Daily Letter. Put the Daily Letter out on a small table by the entrance to the class at the end of each day. If we have the students pick up their copy of the Daily Letter as they come in each morning, they will be ready to begin after recess when it is time to begin the sharing of the Daily Letter. Many of them will be curious to see what the new Daily Letter is about and may choose to read it right then, or they may tuck it in their binders.

Lizzy, a learning disabled student, really struggles with routines. Lizzy can easily get lost in the regular classroom. She has a great deal of difficulty with being on time, having her Daily Letter ready, and getting routines straight.

I like to stand at the door in the morning and welcome Lizzy and all of my other students. If Lizzy comes in late, I can greet her and ask her to bring me her Daily Letter. I monitor her movement and notice that it is very easy for her to be distracted from this one instruction. I know that Lizzy will often forget to take the Daily Letter and notices out of her backpack at school. Lizzy needs gentle reminders to get her things done. As I greet other students, I make sure I move closer to her. I compliment her when she brings her Daily Letter to me.

It may take months for Lizzy to be able to manage this routine. I work hard to help her feel successful in the first moments of the day. It requires time and effort to break down the Daily Letter routine into baby steps and follow them through with her, but it is worth it. I want Lizzy to have a positive experience with her Daily Letter. A good start to Lizzy's day will pay off for those working and playing with her.

Lizzy eventually becomes more comfortable and successful at being able to get her Daily Letter folder out of her backpack and to put her new Daily Letter into it just like everyone else. She also becomes comfortable and successful in her literacy learning setting, and begins to see herself as a more capable student.

Time and Setting

Create a predictable time for the shared Daily Letter learning event.

Time

We can create a powerful story-sharing community by having our students share a Daily Letter experience each school day at the same time. Plan to teach the Daily Letter early in the day. This may be more important when you work with younger students. It is practical to teach the Daily Letter after recess, so there is time for the pre-teaching of at-risk students before recess. It also gives time for follow-up teaching after the whole-group Daily Letter sharing after lunch.

Mary and Marty are middle-of-the-road students. I like to have time for these students to settle in after recess and get ready for the sharing of the Daily Letter. Mary and Marty are independent enough to reread old favorites or look and chat about the newest Daily Letter in the collection. It is Adam's turn to put the Daily Letter on the overhead projector and close the blinds. Everyone gets out their highlighters and checks to see that their group is ready to begin sharing. Mary and Marty are quietly reading while they wait to begin the Daily Letter. I am free to help Annie, an at-risk student who feels left out of a game at recess. I attend to Annie's needs while everyone else settles in for the sharing of the Daily Letter.

When we have finished the Daily Letter, I take a few minutes to quietly compliment Mary and Marty. I want Mary and Marty to know I have noticed that they made good use of their time at the beginning of the Daily Letter and during the sharing of the Daily Letter. I tell them how much I appreciate how their manage their time, and remind them that even though I was busy with Annie, I did notice how independent they were. I take the time to write a short compliment on their Daily Letters. I remind them to show the notes written on the back of their Daily Letter pages to their parents that night.

I am happy to catch students like Mary and Marty doing things right. Predictable times and routines for the Daily Letter make the day run smoothly for everyone. Middle-of-the-road students have a lot to do with carrying out the routines, yet they sometimes go unnoticed. They sometimes get less attention than the at-risk or exceptional students. I want Mary and Marty to know how important they are. If I can enlist the middle-of-the-road students to take responsibility for following the predictable schedule, they will be able to manage the routines of the day and much of their own learning as well.

Attending to Mary and Marty and all the middle-of-the-road students makes the class a better place to be for everyone. I sometimes need to be free to help others with recess problems. I can effectively do this when I share the responsibility for learning with Mary and Marty and the rest of the community of learners.

Create a predictable setting.

Setting

We create a powerful story-sharing community by making the classroom space for the sharing of the Daily Letter predictable. Organize the students to sit in groups of four so they can share their ideas and interests. Choose a place for the author to stand to lead the sharing of the Daily Letter that is in plain view of all the students. Have the overhead projector and charts with prompts for the talk about text in plain view. To have a really useful Word Wall, make it readily accessible below the chalk ledge so that you can walk over and add words to it, or draw attention to it as you study words on the Daily Letter. If the setting is predictable, students can more easily be responsible for maintaining it.

I have Adam in charge of using the overhead projector to track the reading of the Daily Letter. This job engages Adam in the text, and does the same for others. Giving Adam an important job during the Daily Letter assists him to focus and participate responsibly in the routine of the story-sharing community. When he has this space and role during the Daily Letter, his behavior is more focused. This helps the other students to see Adam as a more capable student. I model acceptance of Adam, helping the students notice that he is doing this job well. Adam, as an active, at-risk student, can be woven into the fabric of this capable classroom by employing him to assist with the technology. Adam has a chance to participate positively and have his reputation redefined.

Students can be responsible for organizing the materials, the setting, timing, and the technology to support the learning. Empowering students to manage the routines keeps them involved and gives a wonderful, quiet, "proud to be taking care of business" tone to the class. Students take great pride in being responsible for the learning that takes place.

When you make the Daily Letter a predictable use of time, routines, material, and space, you provide security and comfort for your fledgling learners for when, how, what, and where they will learn. Your students will not be overwhelmed when these aspects of their learning environment are predictable.

It is within these routines the students will have a great deal of freedom to make real choices about their learning on the Daily Letter. As you and your students become more familiar with the daily routines, you will become freer to work on new aspects of your learning as each fresh Daily Letter is shared. The predictability of the Daily Letter is highly conducive to the high-risk activity of sharing what proficient readers and writers do. Keeping the routine deliberate, consistent, and simple each day actually supports the unpredictable and complex business of story-sharing with your students.

CHAPTER 3

The Story-Sharing Community

The outcomes of the learning process for your students will be varied and often unpredictable each year. It is a new and challenging role to begin to live with the ambiguity. Since the students have choice over the subject and format of their Daily Letter learning, you will have to give up a measure of control over both the process and the outcomes. It is equally challenging to live with the idea that our students' interpretations and perspectives of their own Daily Letters may be richer than we could imagine and may take the story-sharing community in numerous, unexpected, zigzagging directions.

The Daily Letter story-sharing community is not static or fixed, but always dynamic, evolving, shifting through the actions and interactions of the community. How to activate the dynamics of the story-sharing community with a set of roles and responsibilities for all your students? What are the roles and responsibilities of the members of the story-sharing community? Here is a list of some of the ways to activate the dynamics of the Daily Letter story-sharing community:

- organize inclusive collaborative learning
- have student learning through leading
- use students as mentors and apprentices
- teacher's role to lead from behind
- inclusive employment of members of the community
- teachers making a difference

Over the school year, you will find that the dynamics of the story-sharing community will shift in several ways:

- From teaching/learning that is solely managed by the teacher ➜ to learning that is managed by both the teacher and students-as-leaders/mentors
- From whole-class teacher-directed instruction ➜ to whole-class student-led instruction
- From teacher-directed instruction ➜ to student-centred learning
- From one-sided teaching where the teacher is responsible for the learning ➜ to shared responsibility of the learning between the student and the teacher
- From the teacher being solely involved in teaching and responsible for learning ➜ to the teacher responding contingently to the learning needs of the community of learners

- From a distant relationship between teacher and students ➡ to a close personal relationship where the teacher is involved with students and the students are involved with teacher
- From teacher-designed text/reading material ➡ to student-designed text created through student inquiry and exploration
- From student passivity (sitting, listening to information) ➡ to the transformation of participation of the students into social and active learners
- From teacher-directed talk about text ➡ to student-centred collaborative talk about text
- From students acting as individual learners ➡ to students participating through assisted social, collaborative action
- From independent student action ➡ to interdependent social interaction
- From a competitive learning model ➡ to a collaborative community of learners

Collaborative Learning

Activate the dynamics of the story sharing community with organized inclusive collaborative learning.

We create a community where the students share the roles and responsibilities for the learning that takes place each time we do the Daily Letter. Activate the dynamics of the community through collaboration with a central purpose, the story-sharing of the Daily Letter.

Use the Daily Letter to nurture the co-construction of knowledge with the mutual engagement of the entire class. Include all learners—from mature to the less mature, from exceptional to at-risk, from English as a first language to English as a second language—in the collaborative creation and sharing of the Daily Letter. Ensure that all students contribute their uniqueness to the group by sharing several of their stories each month. Include all stories—the mature and less mature stories, exceptional and ordinary, English as a first language and English as a second language. Ensure every student is given equal value and membership to bind your class into a community where the expertise, creativity, interests, wisdom, and humor of individual members touch others.

TOP TEN

Book Pick for more information on Community Building:
Tribes by Jeanne Gibbs

Ways to Involve Students in Building the Story-sharing Community

1. share the talents, knowledge, interests of everyone—but never their needs
2. give everyone lots of choice of stories, genres, literacy activities
3. ensure there is no segregation of students
4. give everyone Daily Letter jobs to do collaboratively
5. celebrate the creative efforts and contributions of the community
6. celebrate the message that we all have stories to tell and that the community is stronger and richer with each of our stories
7. have celebrations early on—share food, snacks, luncheons
8. partner students for collaborative activities
9. share free time together
10. go places outside of the school together

Kelvin, a student with English as his second language, is able to share a wealth of creative talents in the classroom and is a valued member of the story-sharing community. He shares a friendship and working partnership with Steven, an outgoing, social, and active member of the writing community.

Steven and Kelvin work collaboratively to prepare a Daily Letter with a set of illustrated origami directions to fold a man's shirt out of paper. Steven and Kelvin practise the steps in the paper-folding demonstration in English. The boys put a tremendous effort into preparing and organizing the materials for their origami Daily Letter. Kelvin leads by reading the instructions on the Daily Letter. Steve demonstrates each fold, and then they both go around and help individuals. The students are highly engaged with this hands-on Daily Letter experience.

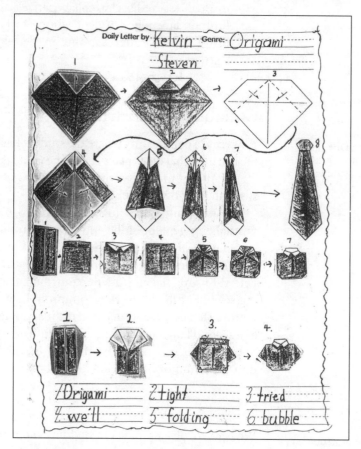

The students are appreciative of Kelvin's efforts to speak English and are attentive to his soft-spoken voice. Everyone ends up with both a paper-folded shirt for a Father's Day gift and respect for the talents of these members of the story-sharing community. This Daily Letter encourages a genuine collaborative partnership and friendship between these two. This Daily Letter engages every member of the story-sharing community.

Embracing the Talents of ESL Students

Do you have a method to integrate your ESL students with others students in the class for their literacy learning? It isn't easy to make ESL students feel they can contribute to the community of learners.

One way to meet this challenge is to have all your students represent their learning in a variety of ways on the Daily Letter. This makes the collaboration between students of diverse backgrounds possible.

The collaborative enterprise of the Daily Letter meets the needs of those students whose literacy experiences do not reflect the school culture's literate forms. With the Daily Letter, students are able to build upon their own sense of identity while still cultivating their emerging literacy abilities. The Daily Letter meets the challenge of creating a community of learners that unites diverse purposes and practices.

Creating the Community

Activate the dynamics of the story-sharing community by introducing the students to the formation of a community to share responsibility with the teacher for the learning that takes place.

It is our first task at the beginning of the year to create the story-sharing community. At the beginning of the year, I find my students will form only a loose network of students without the benefits of the shared practice of the Daily Letter. It is my goal to model the composing and sharing of the Daily Letter and give the students time to participate in these activities.

As we model the shared literacy of the Daily Letter, the students begin to find each other. They discover common ground and begin to develop their shared interests, concerns, and experiences. Encourage your students to find a variety of partners to write Daily Letters with, to explore their shared interests. Gradually introduce them to the idea that they will soon be able to contribute to the shared responsibility for constructing Daily Letters and leading the Daily Letter with the larger community.

It is necessary to provide support to the fledgling contributors in several different ways. These students will need guidance and resources. It is up to you to initiate the cycle, to help them connect their writing experiences to the metacognitive strategies they will share when they teach their Daily Letters. Encourage them to move forward with the ideas that matter most to them, and to contribute by sharing these ideas with the other writers. Watch and listen to your students, and attach them to others who would be suitable to work on collaborative Daily Letter projects.

There are a number of important things I do at the beginning of the year to create the story-sharing community. I begin to stage an awareness campaign about the Daily Letter, and share the benefits and goals of this story-sharing community. I assess and evaluate the students informally and identify the wants and needs of the community. I help the students find common ground through whole-group conversations during the presentations of my read-alouds and Daily Letters. I organize the sharing of my own community-building Daily Letters. I move students around in different partnerships to improve my view of the dynamics of the fledgling story-sharing community.

There are a number of important things I do to facilitate individuals in the story-sharing community. I track the knowledge flow and knowledge relationships within the large group. I begin helping students find other students of like minds, interests, and concerns. I also design and create the support structure for my at-risk or low-progress students. I coach the support staff on the use of the Daily Letter so they may begin the pre-teaching of the Daily Letter to some students. I inform the parents on the use of the Daily Letter in an evening information meeting so they may begin the sharing of the Daily Letter at home each school night.

I begin to impress on the students their need to contribute to the group. As we go along, I discover that many of them want to contribute to their world. They want to make a difference to our learning. When they contribute they bring their own unique abilities to the group. This appears to help all of the story-sharing community succeed.

When students' ideas, interests, and concerns are voiced with the Daily Letter and heard with the sharing of the Daily Letter, we all become more connected and caring about one another. The students bring more of themselves to the class and me, and I bring more of myself to them. With the building of the story-sharing community, each student becomes infinitely more precious to me.

Setting Goals

Activate the dynamics of the story-sharing community by setting goals for shared responsibility for the crafting and teaching of the Daily Letter.

We activate the dynamics of the story-sharing community through setting goals with and for the story-sharing community. We need to carefully prepare to identify the goals of the community with our students.

I set a long-range goal—for my classroom to become a context where everyone works together to learn and where everyone is a resource for everyone else. I gently begin the process of empowering my students with mentoring roles and provide their inclusive employment in the community.

I set another long-range goal—for the story-sharing community to have the students grow in their independence of instruction from me. I plan for their "transformation of participation" (Rogoff et al, 1996), where they will shift their roles from individual, passive learners to social and active leaders of the Daily Letter sharing.

My prime, over-reaching educational goal is for all the students in my care to become more confident, independent, successful readers, writers, listeners, speakers, and thinkers. I want them to become life-long literate beings through their active participation in our unique story-sharing community.

Annie and I work together to set learning goals for the writing and sharing of her Daily Letter. She comes to understand the strengths and weaknesses of her literacy learning as she shares her Daily Letters at weekly workshop conferences with me. As her talents and abilities emerge over the course of the school year, she can set reading, writing, speaking, and leadership goals with each Daily Letter presentation. She is already oriented towards becoming better at talking about each component of her literacy learning after four weeks of goal setting.

As the teacher, I am responsible for instructing Annie in ways to monitor her own developing literacy competencies. I use rubrics with performance standards to provide the language of learning Annie and her parents need, with specific and sufficient feedback on her progress. I show the rubric descriptors, supported with samples of Daily Letters, to Annie so she can set goals for her literacy learning. So far Annie has reached the goals she has set each week and steadily improved her learning.

From Participation to Leadership

Shared Responsibility

Activate the dynamics of the story-sharing community by setting expectations for the shared responsibility for learning in the story-sharing community.

When we see the community of learners begin to settle into the shared routine of the Daily Letter, it is time to make a bigger shift towards sharing the responsibility for the learning between the students and ourselves.

I use the predictable step-by-step routine of the Daily Letter to teach my students how to manage their leading of the Daily Letter. I work hard to have them share read-alouds. Then, after they have learned to effectively select and share read-alouds, I invite them to share Daily Letters they have created. I encourage them to lead a Daily Letter with me. I may choose to involve them in leading one of the think-alouds of the Daily Letter. I train each of the students-as-leaders to be attentive to the ideas and interests of the rest of the children, to listen carefully to what each student will say. Gradually I begin to see an increase in the participation of the discourse community. I affirm that what they have to say and how they choose to say it matters. I nurture their comfortable sense of belonging, which in turn will nurture more lively conversation and risk taking by all.

You must negotiate the roles and responsibilities the students will have when they share a leadership role with you. My goal is to have the students work harder and feel accepted and respected for the new roles and responsibilities they assume. My goal is to encourage them to take risks, contribute new ideas, and make mistakes in a safe supportive story-sharing environment.

There is something richer being cultivated as we share more and more of the leadership role in the classroom. It is a strong character-building time. The students work hard and well together as they get to know each Daily Letter, taking turns and negotiating the meaning of it. The leader learns how to talk about his or her presentation, to clarify and modify his or her demonstration, to talk about the choice of thinking strategies he or she uses. This gives the other students valuable experience in clarifying their choices and decisions, and in the compromise and criticism they will face in both the writing and the presentation of the Daily Letter. This is a context for the sharing of skills of contributing to the group, making group decisions, negotiating text meaning, and getting along! Each apprentice will have many opportunities to play a role in the Daily Letter and learn how ideas are negotiated and problems are solved.

By October we have shared 51 read-alouds and 20 Daily Letters. I breathe a sigh of relief as the students show some very good signs of coming together as a community. The students are comfortable with the predictable daily routine of read-alouds and Daily Letter story sharing. I continue to use routine demonstrations of what good readers and writers do with each component of the Daily Letter. I work hard to engage them in lots of think-alouds about the strategies that make sense of their in-the-head thinking. Numerous charts fill the room with lists of the students' ideas on what good readers, writers, speakers, listeners, and thinkers do.

There is something magical about the students taking the big step towards having full responsibility for the creating and sharing of the Daily Letter. They are building their own strong sense of place in the story-sharing community as they share more and more of the leadership roles. It doesn't take long before I can feel that the community actively takes charge of its story-sharing practice and grows through their sharing of new roles and responsibilities each day. They are beginning to recognize their potential as leaders of the story-sharing community.

As more and more of the students take on the role to lead the Daily Letter, I notice they are beginning to work together more effectively in partners and small groups to produce a wide variety of genres for their Daily Letters. They are engaged in many joint ventures to create interesting and informative demonstrations of their Daily Letters. They are also developing a sense of commitment and closer working relationships with each other, their parents (as a viable audience), and me. The students are empowered with this challenge to share their best approximations of adult texts and the practices that go into both making them and teaching them. They see themselves, and present themselves, as authors, as illustrators, and especially as responsible leaders.

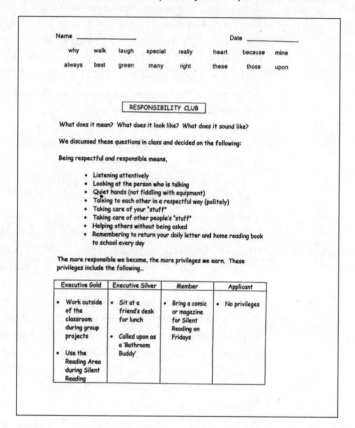

By October I am already noticing that the writers of Daily Letter are enjoying their writing more and more. They are becoming more and more conscious of their own lives as writers. They seem to easily share more, feel more, think more, and learn more about more things. When the students become more empowered this way (as literate persons), they begin to take more chances. They also develop their ideas more, and become more attentive to what they are doing. They do more dreaming and planning together with one another. Sharing Daily Letters is an engaging way for students to show that they are both knowledgeable and in charge of their own learning (perhaps their own lives).

The reason the quality of the writing changes dramatically in the classroom may be that my students have a much better sense of what good readers, writers, listeners, and speakers do. The quality of the story writing and sharing seems to improve as the tone, values, and relationships grow and change. As the social climate settles, the students begin to accept one another and share concerns and respect for one another. They begin to feel safe in the story-sharing community.

Transformation of Participation

We nurture a powerful collaborative story-sharing community by finally handing over responsibilities for the leading of the whole Daily Letter event to our students. It will usually be some time in October that you will make the move to hand control of the Daily Letter over to the students who are ready to accept it. Encourage them to make choices and share their ideas on their sharing of each of the components of the Daily Letter. Be particularly attentive as you oversee and support them through their first presentations. Set and maintain clear, explicit expectations about the roles and responsibilities of the members of the story-sharing community.

The handing over of the teaching of the Daily Letter is an important milestone in the students' growing independence and power. When I invite my students to develop a sense of power to teach their own lesson on literacy, I invite them to learn through leadership. To feel powerful in the story-sharing community, students need to believe that what they teach is useful to others and that what they learn is useful to themselves. They learn that the choices they make in how to teach their Daily Letter contributes to the success of themselves and the others in the community. They become aware of themselves as readers and writers, speakers and listeners responsible for creating and sharing quality work.

Alison is an exceptional reader. She has an extensive collection of books at home and agrees to share her favorite book, *Matilda* by Roald Dahl, with the class. Alison's mother, a master teacher herself, has equipped her daughter with a repertoire of read-aloud skills second to none for our first student-led read-aloud of the year.

Alison's choice of this novel commits her to a week of read-alouds. With each chapter she reads, the students are mesmerized by her cast of delightful voices. Students flock to the library and bookstore to get copies of anything written by Roahl Dahl as a result of Alison's amazing read-aloud.

Matilda Response
by R. Dahl
Response by Alison

I think this book is a wonderful inspiring book because even though Matilda has bad parents she grows up to be an outstanding intelligent adult.

I think this book is for children ages 8-11 because it has in between words and size of printing.

It begins with Matilda having very bad parents but surprisingly enough she is an unbelievable child with her math and language arts. She is in first grade and her teacher is very inspired by her. She has the worst principal and she is still intelligent despite all the bad things that her parents and the bad principal do to her. She gets back at them in hilarious ways.

This is a nonfiction story book because it involves a little bit of magic and a lot of nonfiction text. My opinion of this book is that it is a wonderful, inspiring, intelligent, outstanding book because all these wonderful parts put together make a great big wonderful text. It had good phrases like she had "beautiful glittering eyes" and "big yummy chocolate cake".

This connects to my life because, just like Matilda, I have had wonderful teachers for three grades.

This book relates to a couple of other books I have read which are George's Marvellous Medicine and The Twits by R. Dahl. Both of these books are hilarious and you will notice that in some of R. Dahl's other books, including these ones, involve a few mean people.

Other books by R. Dahl:
The BFG
James and the Giant Peach
The Twits
George's Marvellous Medicine
The Witches
Charlie and the Chocolate Factory
The Wonderful Story of Henry Sugar
Charlie and the Great Glass Elevator
Boy
Danny Champion of the World
Going Solo
Fantastic Mr. Fox
The Magic Finger
The Giraffe, the Pelly and Me
The Enormous Crocodile
Revolting Rhymes
Dirty Beasts

Alison also writes a Daily Letter to go with her Roahl Dahl read-aloud. She chooses to write a personal response to the book. Instead of a poem on the back of the Daily Letter Alison provides a long list of her favorite books by this author. I am pleased that Alison and the rest of the community have spent time on persuasive writing. This is an important genre for students to become familiar with for their future critical literacy learning

---

Have you ever put a student in the role of sharing a read aloud or telling a story? This can be a powerful opportunity for a student to shine. It is really important that the student takes seriously the role to lead the read-aloud. This read-aloud needs be practised to perfection at home. You can check to see that the story reader is well prepared to share a lively introduction and well practised to share a polished reading of a book of his or her choice before reading it to the story-sharing community.

Eventually other students can be put in charge of finding a good read-aloud to go along with their Daily Letter. Students take this invitation to heart and are empowered when given the responsibility to select a suitable one that will fit with their audience and is connected to their Daily Letter. Angel's wonderful parody "Ghostylox and the Three Vampires" was preceded by a read aloud of Goldilocks and the Three Bears and a string of Halloween books. Members of the reading audience can then be invited to search out other versions of these stories as well. The invitation to write in the style of a story is much more seductive if the students are immersed in a number of versions of that story.

My role in the community of story-sharing is to do only those things that Adam cannot do for himself. I do not want to give an impression that I am bigger, more capable, more experienced, or more knowing than any other member of the community. Having Adam do what he can for himself empowers him to experience his own abilities as a reader, writer, speaker, and listener. I can show trust in his abilities as a leader of the Daily Letter. He develops a sense of well-being based on the realization that he is capable of meeting and solving problems as a literacy learner, and develops self-efficacy through sharing this as the student-as-leader of the Daily Letter. I want to show respect for him as a capable learner and leader.

Students who can read, can lead a read-aloud. Students can run the overhead projector, can run a computer presentation, and can write on the chalkboard in big letters like the teacher. They can lead the dictation of a set of words from the text, and go around and check to see if it has been copied carefully. They can select, talk about, and read good books out loud. They can write on chart paper to keep lists and work at the Word Wall if their teacher believes in the shared responsibility for learning and chooses to take the time to teach them how to do it.

Have you ever noticed how the most expert teacher is busy managing the class while the most at-risk students are learning from the least expert adult in the room (often a volunteer or assistant)? What is the most important role of the teacher? What I do, that my students and assistants can't, is work with the most at-risk individuals who need the most strategic, important, expert counsel over their learning. This is what I have the training to do. This is what I love to do. This is what they need me to do. Students are perfectly capable of doing much of the everyday classroom management themselves. This frees me up to work for short periods of time with the students who need me the most.

Daily Letters that Mentor the Creation of New Daily Letters

1. Daily Letters about the same author or illustrator
2. Daily Letters connected to a school, grade, or class theme
3. Daily Letters connected to a style
4. Daily Letters connected to a concept
5. Daily Letters connected to the culture
6. Daily Letters with other information about the topic
7. non-fiction information related to the story on the Daily Letter
8. fiction related to the non-fiction information on the Daily Letter
9. related stories written by others in the story-sharing community
10. reviews, reports, or articles related to the Daily Letter story or its setting or time period.

Leadership

> Learning and leading cannot be separated, leading is a form of learning together. Instructional programs that evoke student voice, apply the principles of constructivism, attend to intrinsic motivation, build resiliency, and engage students in democratic governance—all within a small context, whether natural or contrived—develop the leadership capacity of students. (Lambert, p. 64)

Activate the dynamics of the story-sharing community with students learning through leading the Daily Letter.

We create an environment that nurtures students-as-leaders when we implement the role of student-as-teacher of the Daily Letter. Student leading of the Daily Letter offers substantial opportunities for learning through leadership. Give the message to all students that they can lead the sharing of the Daily Letter because there is something special about them and that they have many stories to tell. With this belief, their learning will likely become more deeply intertwined with their leading of the Daily Letter. Affirm students are capable, literate persons, well able to be in charge of the learning of the larger community from time to time. Make sure they understand that their leading of the Daily Letter is the public expression of their literacy learning, and that you are proud that each one of them can learn and every one of them can lead (Lambert, 2003).

Place students, one at a time, in this learning-through-leading role with their Daily Letters. Cultivate student leadership to advance the learning of both the leaders and the story-sharing community.

TOP TEN

Characteristics of Leaders of the Daily Letter

1. assertive behavior
2. good body language—proper stance, facing students
3. appropriate facial expressions
4. appropriate distance for leading
5. appropriate tone of voice
6. active listening to students
7. leading is connected to increased achievement
8. shared leadership roles are encouraged
9. leadership skills are assessed with rubrics
10. all students are given leadership roles

Each year that I have used the Daily Letter, I have been able to give every child the right, the responsibility, and the capability to be a leader. Even my most at-risk, ESL, learning-disabled, autistic students have chosen to present their Daily Letter to the class. These children have taught me how students can provide powerful modeling of support for one another in various roles of the story-sharing community.

Allen is an autistic, learning-disabled ESL student who wants to share his Daily Letter with the class. Allen loves books and selects one to talk about on his Daily Letter. His favorite book, *Armadillo Rodeo* by Jan Brett, is the story of an armadillo that falls in love with a pair of cowboy boots. Allen's teaching assistant helps Allen prepare for his Daily Letter sharing by scripting what he will say about each component of his Daily Letter and practising it several times beforehand. When I introduce Allen to the class, he refuses to follow the script. He also refuses any help from anyone to lead the sharing of his Daily Letter.

I cross my fingers and step back as Allen addresses the students by name and asks them to share their ideas. In his four years of schooling, Allen has never made eye contact with any of the students or called them by name. This is a wondrous, remarkable event, with Allen learning by leading. At the end of the Daily Letter, some of the students spontaneously respond to Allen's remarkable performance, only to be respectfully silenced by other students who remember how sensitive Allen is to noise.

I am rendered speechless by Allen's marvelous interaction with his peers. Allen goes on to share more Daily Letters with the class this year.

Armadillo Rodeo   By: Jan Brett

I recommend this book to intermediate students because the vocabulary is more difficult.

Bo, the armadillo was picking the flowers when he saw a lizard. He became separated from his mother when he saw Harmony Jean wearing red boots. Bo thought these boots were red armadillo. He followed the boots into the water, then to the Curly H ranch where the rodeo was taking place. Then he found bright-green jalapeno pepper and it was so hot he drank some lemonade. After The Dance, Harmony took out her boots and the Armadillo talk to the boots. The boots said, "Nothing.   Armadillo said, Armadilloooooooo!

This is a fiction book because Armadillos do not talk, Armadillos do not pick flowers, Armadillos do not ride a horse.

This connects to my life because I got lost once · I was very little when it happened.

The best part for me was when Bo found a bright green jalapeno pepper and drinking the lemonade. It is very hot I know.

Vocabulary; there are some rodeo words such as boots, Curly H, (ranch) pardner, fiddle and cowhands.

Apprenticeship and Mentorship

Activate the dynamics of the story-sharing community with apprenticeship and mentorship roles.

We activate the dynamics of the story-sharing community by engaging our students in mentoring and apprenticing roles. Create and nurture a strong interdependent community where each member can help/learn with each other in a purposeful, practical mentoring and apprenticing community.

The apprentices in the story-sharing community are all the students participating in the constructing and sharing of the Daily Letter. Students, as apprentices, are not learning just through observing and imitation. They gain a variety of insights from collaborating in the composing of Daily Letters. They gain more insights from the connections and understandings expressed by other leaders of the Daily Letters as their mentors, and from their own leading. They learn by participating in both roles in the story-sharing community, both absorbing and being absorbed into the community.

As the apprentices gradually assemble an idea of what it means to be a good reader, writer, listener, speaker, and thinker, they can take their ideas from each Daily Letter and apply them to future Daily Letters. This knowledge gained can, in turn, be applied to new situations outside of the classroom as part of their life-long learning.

Adam has an advantage. Adam mesmerizes his friends with his showmanship in his leadership of his Daily Letter. Although Adam may struggle to get his ideas down on paper to compose his Daily Letter, he has a great advantage when leading the sharing of his Daily Letter. His strong verbal capabilities and stage presence are obvious.

As part of his shared responsibility for the leading to learn the Daily Letter, Adam decides he wants to ensure that everyone has an equal chance to stand and talk about the text as we code it. Adam develops a methodical system of selecting volunteers to share from each group. He systematically picks each student to share until everyone has been chosen. He thoughtfully does this to ensure that everyone gets a fair chance to talk about their ideas on the Daily Letter.

Adam is a caring eight-year-old, and he tries hard to include everyone in the talk about text. Many other students adopt his systematic way of calling on students. He can be proud of his sense of fairness, a quality recognized by the members of the story-sharing community. I make a note—a compliment—on Adam's Daily Letter, sharing examples of his social responsibility with his parents.

When my students have a shared responsibility to manage the Daily Letter, they seen to fall into a role as engaged, thoughtful, and reflective mentors to the apprenticing literacy learners. Having students replicate the sharing of their own Daily Letter strategies each day is far from boring for my students. Many of them depend on the routine and take pleasure in the sameness of it. The demonstrations of thinking strategies themselves, however, are seldom the same. We delight as a story-sharing community in the variation of choice of topic, format, and strategy sharing each mentor brings to the story-sharing forum.

Inclusive Membership

We nurture a powerful collaborative story-sharing community by employing many of the members of the group during the *sharing* of the Daily Letter. Employ everyone by systematically rotating through all the jobs in the class.

We nurture a powerful collaborative story-sharing community by employing many of the members of the group during the *creating* of the Daily Letter. Plan for the students to edit and proof each other's stories and poems, and to do the final checklist to see if the Daily Letter is ready for publishing. Have some students go with a parent to photocopy their Daily Letters and make the overhead transparencies. Enlist a student to organize the sign-up sheet for sharing the Daily Letter.

Roles and Responsibilities in the Story-sharing Community

Role	Responsibility
Leader	sharing the Daily Letter: each component/strategy
Chair	reviewing the Daily Letter with individuals after the whole group
Mentor	sharing the Daily Letter (after centres)
Co-Leader	assisting the Leader with the delivery of the Daily Letter
Co-Chair	reviewing the Daily Letter with individuals after the whole group
Co-Mentor	sharing the Daily Letter
Technology Assistants	using the overhead projector or computer display software to support the use of hard copy of the Daily Letter by individual students
Word Wall Assistants	overseeing the addition of words to the Word Wall during the Daily Letter Coding of the Text strategy
Tracking Assistant	going around and assisting students as they follow along with the Daily Letter
Marking Assistant	supporting the Leader by going around and checking each student's Written Word Study and Reader Response

Do you have jobs in your class related to keeping the class clean and organized? Are your students keen to do these jobs? Are they capable of doing these jobs? What happens if you give students jobs related to their own learning and understanding? Would they rise to the occasion with these roles as well?

TOP TEN

Roles of the Daily Letter Story-sharing Community

1. each student becomes the leader of the Daily Letter sharing each month
2. each student becomes co-leader of the Daily Letter sharing
3. two technology persons: run overhead together
4. editors and proofreaders: edit and proofread work during workshop
5. peer tutor: review past Daily Letters with students selected by the teacher
6. technical support: run copies/make overheads of the Daily Letters
7. computer monitors: help students working on the computer
8. teacher: circulate to support, compliment students
9. Word Wall wizard: manage the Word Wall
10. assessors: evaluate reader responses with performance standards (class-designed rubric or formal district-developed rubric)

Role of the Teacher

As the teacher, you are ultimately responsible for the student's immersion in read-alouds, the sharing of the Daily Letter, and the individual/group shared responsibilities for the learning that takes place with the story-sharing community. You need to be adaptable to manage this complex, messy learning environment for students. Remain committed to the belief that in order to cultivate story-sharing in the classroom, you have to work hard to create and nurture a community where each of the members becomes more and more committed to the collaborative co-construction of knowledge. Your role over the year will be to respond contingently by assisting students when needed or to withdraw and hand over control whenever students show themselves capable of proceeding independently. Encourage the community of learners to seek solutions to their own problems and use their peers as an important resource for learning.

Your role is that of a coach or consultant rather than a director or sole bearer of the information. A student who is empowered to be in control of his or her own learning, who knows why reading and writing is important and what needs to be done to improve it, is more likely to engage in the kinds of repeated practice that leads to improved standing.

Activate the dynamics of the story-sharing community through principled eclecticism.

TOP TEN

Shifts in the Role of the Teacher

1. lead but respond
2. inform but listen
3. instruct but collaborate
4. evaluate but teach
5. demonstrate but participate
6. organize but become involved
7. manage but support
8. model but assist
9. confer but observe
10. criticize but appreciate

(adapted from Booth, 2001, p. 9)

Leading From Behind

Activate the dynamics of the story-sharing community with the role of the teacher being that of leading from behind.

Overall, it is your responsibility as the teacher to create, nurture, and sustain the story-sharing community over the year. However, this role will change drastically as you learn to lead more and more from behind.

Sometime in the late fall or early spring, the community will become well established. Many of the students will find their voices as leaders and mentors, and will gain influence over the apprentice writers. Many of our children engaged in the joint activities of the Daily Letter, creating and sharing Daily Letters, will become more adaptable with the changing circumstances of each shared learning experience.

As the teacher of this dynamic story-sharing community you move gradually more and more to the periphery of the Daily Letter sharing. When you give control of the learning operation over to students-as-leaders, they are in control of sharing each component of their Daily Letter. While you are never far away, you seldom take direct action in the students' investigation of the text. Be there to answer questions, should they arise, or deal with a crisis; otherwise, do not intervene to direct what the students are learning. In giving them the responsibility to create and take on the challenges of leading the talk about text and the strategies they use, you provide the conditions in which they grow in personal confidence. It empowers your students to take responsibility for leading to learn.

TOP TEN

Strategies to Build a Strong Teacher–Student Relationship

1. Use appropriate levels of dominance.
2. Set clear, purposeful guidelines for the behavior of the community.
3. Set clear, purposeful academic guidelines.
4. Provide teacher guidance.
5. Be assertive about appropriate behavior.
6. Set clear rules, procedures, and routines.
7. Monitor general and individual behavior.
8. Monitor group behavior; monitor transitions.
9. Set clear guidelines about interruptions.
10. Set routines around the materials and equipment of the classroom.

The Daily Letter Home Program

Ownership involves a students' valuing of reading and writing at home as well as at school (Au, 1993). Students with ownership use literacy for their own purposes and in the everyday parts of their lives. We cannot consider students skillful readers if they only read for school ssignments and never read for their own enjoyment or information.

The Daily Letter encourages proficiency and purposeful self-motivated learning, especially if a snippet of a good story is on the Daily Letter. The taking of the Daily Letter home each night encourages students to discuss something they learned at school that day with family members. When students engage in discussions around literacy each night with parents, they gain practice and confidence at expressing themselves more freely. This kind of dynamic discussion is made available to the parent and child with the Daily Letter. The student has ownership of the Daily Letter and can become more and more skilled at sharing their literacy learning with others.

I see a powerful partnership created between the school and the home with the Daily Letter, as it goes back and forth each day with the students. Parents, students, and the teacher can conveniently pass along comments, compliments, and questions in the space provided on the back of the Daily Letter.

With practice, students can learn to effectively explain what they did that day by sharing their Daily Letter with their parents routinely each night. The themes, genres, and special events of their day come alive for the parents through this brief sharing of the Daily Letter. The Daily Letter conveniently assists parents in becoming partners in their children's education.

A classic question from a parent to their child is, "What did you do at school today?" The classic response remains, "Nothing." Do you have a convenient method to assist your students and parents communicate about their life at

With the facilitating of a story-sharing community, I no longer stand up in front of the classroom for long periods of time. I do, however, spend my time working with a variety of individual learners. I don't stay up all night making materials. I may stay up half the night reading their stories.

Create a strong home–school connection.

school? Use the prompt on the bottom of the Daily Letter to provide a starting point for some sort of a dialogue between the parent and child about something they did at school that day. Use the Ask me... prompt to improve the communication between the school and the home and a partnership between the teacher, student, and parent where learning matters. (See BLM #7 page 61.)

ESL Students at Home

English as a Second Language students learn to read and write in a second language with the DL. They also build reading and writing abilities by working through the Daily Letter at night with a parent in their first language. Parents working with their children in both languages is a realistic goal with the Daily Letter.

The Daily Letter sharing takes place each day with the class at school, and each night with the families at home, so that students and parents come to know it so well that it becomes a part of them. The Daily Letter is an important daily event to forge connections between family life, school, community, and culture.

unity partners share learn community love guidance

Unity

I dreamed I stood in a studio
And watched two sculptors there
The clay they used was a young child's mind
And they fashioned it with care.
One was a teacher - the tools she used
Were books, music and art.
The other a parent, worked with a guiding hand
And a gentle, loving heart.
Day after day, the teacher worked with touch
That was deft and sure.
While the parent standing by her side
Polished and smoothed it o'er.
And when at last the task was done
They were proud of what they had wrought.
For the things they had molded into the child
Could neither be sold nor bought.
And each agreed they would have failed
If each had worked alone,
For behind the parent stood the school
And behind the teacher, the home.

Author Unknown

Ask me to tell you about the importance of a partnership between school and home.

Parents and Spelling

Learning to spell is a developmental process that goes from approximations to conventional spelling. Teachers often overvalue spelling programs and undervalue the role of reading and writing in the learning of spelling. Reading and writing are the most important ways to get a student to learn to spell. A student will learn many words by seeing them and playing with them over and over on the Daily Letter.

Spelling is often an issue with teachers because spelling is an issue with parents. Sending eight words home each night (40 words per week) as the Writing Word Study on the back of the Daily Letter is one way to fend off parents while you begin to educate them in the research findings about spelling. The Daily Letter assists a student informally learn spelling patterns, prefixes and suffixes, and unique words.

The spelling list of eight words can be informally reviewed nightly by the parent and child. There is no need for formal spelling tests with the Daily Letter program. Assessment of spelling can be done through analysis of the drafts of the letter. Specific spelling intervention and strategic teaching can be done during conferences in writer's workshop or centre time. Students should spend no more than 10 to 15 minutes per day on spelling.

Nurturing Story-sharing in the Home

We create a powerful story-sharing community by having the Daily Letter go home each night with students to their parents. The family becomes another story-sharing community, and students are engaged in one more sharing of the Daily Letter. They can proudly show and tell what they have learned that day with their parents. Parents are conveniently informed about how their child's day was. Parents can view the progress their child is making in their reading and writing first-hand. They become aware of their child's growing abilities.

Make homework manageable each night by assigning all students to share their Daily Letter each night with their parents. Since the Daily Letter covers the essential components of a comprehensive language arts program, it is a convenient ready-made package of the literacy learning of the day for the parents and student to review each night. Use the Daily Letter as a practical means to alleviate the frustration parents feel in trying to help their child with an assignment that they neither understand nor have the resources to complete.

Annie's parents have agreed to work with Annie and her Daily Letter at night for a trial one-week period. I remind them that their time in the evening working with Annie should be a 15-minute review of the Daily Letter, since she has already worked with it extensively at school. She will have the text to read, a word list to read, and a spelling list of six to eight words to write. She will have a prompt to respond to. She will have graphics and a poem to examine and a written reflection to share.

Annie's parents grow to appreciate the Daily Letter as a convenient means to review Annie's ongoing literacy learning. The routine is helpful to them all. For Annie and her parents, the Daily Letter becomes their first experience of homework without tears.

The Daily Letter, as homework, matters to Annie because it makes her feel successful. She has been well prepared to proudly share her Daily Letter at home. She works hard during the day and can perform many parts of it with ease and pride.

The Daily Letter also matters to Annie's parents because they have an efficient and effective, stress-free strategy to help their daughter with purposeful reading and writing activities. They see the benefit of this time spent together.

This home–school connection matters to me because I have supportive parents as partners working with me, contributing to Annie's growth as a student in a way that that I could not accomplish alone. The Daily Letter matters to all of us as a powerful home–school connection.

Parents can be instructed how to do shared reading at the beginning of the year at a special evening Parent's Meeting. Students who do not yet have the ability to read the Daily Letter can listen to the poem read aloud by the parent or caregiver.

Try inviting parents, teaching assistants, the learning assistant teacher, ESL teachers, administration, etc., to an evening meeting without students, to introduce them to the Daily Letter. Bring everyone on board with the timing, routines, and materials of the Daily Letter. Organizing one evening meeting early in the school year might be worth its weight in gold in forging a strong partnership to nurture the fledgling story-sharing community. Try doing a Daily Letter with them!

TOP TEN

Things to Share at a Daily Letter Parent's Meeting

1. Go over the routine of the Daily Letter going back and forth to school each day.
2. Ask parents to read the Daily Letter each night with their children.
3. Ask parents to initial the back of the Daily Letter page to confirm that they have read it with their children.
4. Ask parents to get a substitute (a babysitter, sibling) to do the Daily Letter if they can't.
5. Take a half-hour and do a Daily Letter with the Parents so they can experience it.
6. Ask for volunteers to help with the computer work to publish Daily Letters.
7. Ask parents to write with their children and make Daily Letters together.
8. Ask parents to practise with their children when it is their turn to share their Daily Letters with the class.
9. Ask parents to communicate with you on the Comments part of the Daily Letter.
10. Encourage parents to write compliments on the Daily Letter page for their child.

Convenient Communication With Parents

We create a powerful story-sharing community by immersing our students in regular communication about their needs and wants. Having a convenient place for short messages on the Daily Letter can provide valuable information that may be helpful in taking care of a student's special needs.

Christina showed me her Daily Letter book, tapping softly on the comment. I braced myself for the remainder of the sadly unspoken news. The comment about the Rogers' old family dog was short and sweet…and important. *Biscuit died during the night* was all it said.

"Too sad to put to words," I whispered quietly as I gave her a soft hug. Her head tipped in agreement as she turned towards the cloakroom. I decided to save the talk for later.

Towards the end of the day I composed a brief message of condolence on the Comment section of the Daily Letter page. It spoke of my sorrow for the news of the passing of their treasured Labrador Retriever. My brief comment also recounted Christina's day and noted that the accompanying book — *Dog Heaven*—might be of interest to Christina and her sister on a future date.

Several weeks later Christina bravely went on to write and share a touching Daily Letter about her old pal Biscuit. Christina also shared the book *Dog Heaven* with the class. She introduced the book as a story that had helped her and her sister Samantha as they suffered through their first days and nights without their beloved Biscuit.

So it goes with the Daily Letter as a communication book between parent, student, and teacher. In times when we just don't have enough time to say everything we would, should, or could, it is nice to have a convenient way to keep home and school lives tightly connected.

TOP TEN

Demonstrations by Students and Parents to Further Develop Community

1. cooking demonstrations
2. science demonstrations: experiments, questions
3. artifact sharing, history demonstrations
4. arts and craft demonstrations
5. buddy activities: big buddies, little buddies, or high school buddies
6. math demonstrations
7. field trips/walking tours: plays, outings, fine arts events, movies
8. guests, visitors, pet parades
9. school events: Hat Day, Pajama Day, Twin Day, Famous Person Day
10. sporting demonstrations, sporting events

Checklist for Sharing the Daily Letter at Home

1. Introduction
   - ❏ Sit together with a parent to share your copy of the Daily Letter.
   - ❏ Read and talk about the author, title, and genre.

2. Before Reading
   - ❏ Pick out difficult words in the text.
   - ❏ Talk about ways to read unfamiliar words in the text.

3. Reading
   - ❏ Read the Daily Letter with or to your parent.

4. After Reading
   - ❏ Look at the highlighted/coded text.
   - ❏ Talk about some of the text that is coded.

5. Reading Word Study
   - ❏ Say the words in the list fast.
   - ❏ Tell your parent some of the strategies good readers use to read these words.

6. Ask Me… prompt
   - ❏ Have your parent read the Ask me… prompt.
   - ❏ Tell them your ideas on this.

7. Writing Word Study
   - ❏ Guided Writing: Have your parent dictate to you the 6 to 8 the words printed on the lines on the back of the Daily Letter.
   - ❏ Close your eyes and spell them or write them down.
   - ❏ Tell your parent the strategies good writers use to write the words.

8. Shared Reading
   - ❏ Read the poem, chant, or song to or with your parent.
   - ❏ Have your parent read and talk about the poem with you.

9. Shared Writing
   - ❏ Read what you have written on the space on the bottom of the page.
   - ❏ Tell your parent about your ideas here.
   - ❏ Have your parent compose, with your help, a compliment or a message to the teacher to put on the space provided on the back of the Daily Letter.

10. Shared Reading
    - ❏ Have your parent read a book or go back through your Daily Letter book and read your favorite ones.

CHAPTER 4

Planning a Daily Letter Program

We can create a powerful story-sharing program by planning and organizing a social and active Daily Letter literacy event each day. However, the actual learning that takes place will remain unknown until the community begin to share stories. Until the interests, concerns, and talents of the group show themselves, you can only prepare the predictable learning environment and wait patiently for the story-sharing community to assemble.

Prepare your Daily Letter program to have students participate in a wide variety of communication skills. Plan to have students engage in a collaborative program with lots of active learning. Ensure it is an inclusive program for all at-risk, learning-disabled, ESL, and low-progress students. This program suits resources people working with all students at one time or another. Arrange for the Daily Letter program to be predictable in the time, routine, materials, and setting. Create a routine for informal assessment during the school day that covers each of the components of a comprehensive literacy-learning plan.

When the students arrive, involve them in the Daily Letter as part of a complex, shared language experience that invites them to participate as both apprentices and mentors. In this kind of a balanced literacy plan, invite students to have a strong voice in many aspects of their school life. With these conditions in place, you are on our way to creating an engaging, exciting story-sharing program that matters to students, parents, and you.

TOP TEN

Ways to Build Community at the Beginning of the School Year
1. interviews and questionnaires with community members
2. introductions of community members as very important persons
3. creation of personal shields of the lives of the community members
4. creation of road maps of the lives of the community members
5. surveys/graphs of aspects of the community's life
6. sharing of the interests of the community's life together
7. sharing of the expertise of the members of the community
8. stories of the lives of the members of the community
9. stories of the families and friends of the community
10. sharing of the students' self-selected inquiries and explorations

The Shape of the Day

The Daily Letter is one important component of a comprehensive language arts program. It represents the large group activity that places all students together to learn about literacy. Use the Daily Letter to share the big ideas of literacy that will be monitored and adjusted within small groups throughout the year.

The Daily Letter is not meant to be used in isolation. The thinking and learning strategies, text organization, and word study focused on in the large group can be revisited and reflected upon by students in the smaller group setting of writer's workshop or centres. Students should participate in many literacy experiences, such as shared language and read-alouds that support the topics of the Daily Letters. They also need to participate in literacy centres, such as reader's theatre, Word Wall activities, guided reading/writing, and independent reading/writing activities. Students can create their Daily Letters during literacy centres or a writer's workshop. They can attend individual conferences during centres/workshop time as well.

At-risk, low-progress students can participate in small-group or one-to-one sessions with you or with a member of your education team, such as the learning assistant or ESL teacher. Students can then review and celebrate their day's accomplishments at home with their families.

The Daily Letter can be used to shape a school day and literacy learning at home, following a rough schedule like the following (see BLM #8 page 65 for a more detailed look):

Morning	Afternoon	Evening
• Read-aloud (language experience) • Intervention: pre-teaching of the Daily Letter to at-risk students • Daily Letter sharing	• Read-aloud (language experience) • Literacy centres and/or workshop for Daily Letters	• At-home sharing of the Daily Letter • At-home choice reading

TOP TEN

Things to Remember when Organizing the Shape of the Day

1. Use whole-group instruction for the sharing of the Daily Letter.
2. Empower students to lead the whole-group instruction by sharing their own read-alouds and Daily Letters when they are ready.
3. Use short-term small groups or partnerships to compose stories and Daily Letters.
4. Involve other support staff in working with students and making decisions about students.
5. Provide in-class instruction for at-risk students by involving support staff in working with them.
6. Deliver high-quality instruction yourself to the low-progress students.
7. Use heterogeneous cooperative writing groups and partnerships to produce Daily Letters.
8. Give students opportunities to work with a number of different students in the class.

Book Pick for more information on Teaching Writing:
The Art of Teaching Writing by Lucy McCormick Calkins

9. Address Individual learning needs with one-on-one instruction during centres or workshop.
10. Review and adjust groups often.

We used the Daily Letter to look at stories about scars, building around Kevin's Daily Letter.

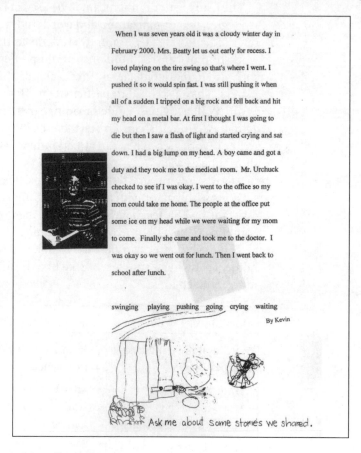

When I was seven years old it was a cloudy winter day in February 2000. Mrs. Beatty let us out early for recess. I loved playing on the tire swing so that's where I went. I pushed it so it would spin fast. I was still pushing it when all of a sudden I tripped on a big rock and fell back and hit my head on a metal bar. At first I thought I was going to die but then I saw a flash of light and started crying and sat down. I had a big lump on my head. A boy came and got a duty and they took me to the medical room. Mr. Urchuck checked to see if I was okay. I went to the office so my mom could take me home. The people at the office put some ice on my head while we were waiting for my mom to come. Finally she came and took me to the doctor. I was okay so we went out for lunch. Then I went back to school after lunch.

swinging   playing   pushing   going   crying   waiting

By Kevin

Ask me about some stories we shared.

Morning

Language Experience
Do you have a scar story to tell?
Story-telling about our scars. Everyone has a story to tell. (10 min.)
Read-aloud
Excerpt from Harry Potter book about the scar on his forehead. (20 min.)
↓
Daily Letter: Kevin
Kevin's Scar Story (60 minutes)

Afternoon

Language Experience
Short sharing of more student scar, hospital stories.
Read-aloud
Mr. Bump by Roger Hargreaves (20 minutes)
↓
Centres/Workshop
Journals/Daily Letters: Draft scar stories or work on choice Daily Letter construction.
Poetry Centre: Shel Silverstein poetry books
Word Wall: -*ar* words (using the car tool)
Reader's Theatre: *Mr. Men* stories

The Shape of the Daily Letter Day

Morning

Language Experience/Read-aloud
Listening to Daily Letter stories

1. author introduction
2. genre introduction
3. pre-reading strategy
4. read-aloud
5. during-reading strategy
6. post-reading strategy
7. visual literacy
8. word study
9. reader response (oral)

Intervention
Daily Letter work with
at-risk readers

1. author introduction
2. genre introduction
3. pre-reading strategy
4. reading of Daily Letter text
5. during-reading strategy
6. coding strategy
7. visual literacy
8. word study
9. reader response (oral)

Daily Letter Sharing

1. author introduction
2. genre introduction
3. pre-reading strategy
4. reading of Daily Letter text
5. during-reading strategy
6. coding strategy
7. visual literacy
8. word study
9. reader response (oral)

Afternoon

Language Experience/Read-aloud
Listening to stories:
1. author introduction
2. genre introduction
3. pre-reading strategy
4. read-aloud
5. during reading strategy
6. post-reading strategy
7. visual literacy
8. word study
9. reader response (oral)

Literacy Centres and/or Workshop
Creating Daily Letters
1. discover subject/topic
2. sense your audience
3. search for specifics
4. create a design
5. write
6. develop a critical eye
7. rewrite
8. assemble Daily Letter
9. prepare to share Daily Letter

Evening

Sharing at Home
Celebrating/rereading Daily Letter
1. author introduction
2. genre introduction
3. reading of text
4. visual literacy
5. word study
6. Ask Me… prompt
7. comments
8. word study
9. poetry reading
10. reader response (oral)

Choice Reading

Evening	**At Home Sharing of the Daily Letter**
	Kevin's Daily Letter
	Ask Me... prompt on the Daily Letter
	Ask me about some stories we shared.
	↓
	Choice Home Reading
	Recommended write: personal narrative
	Recommended read: Harry Potter books; Shel Silverstein poetry; *Mr. Men* books

Intervention

> Learning requires effort and courage. Having teachers and peers respect their ideas in the same forum and formats as all children, makes the effort worthwhile for students with disabilities. The lines between general education and special education are blurring, and we have much to learn from each other. (Scala, p. 10)

We create a powerful story-sharing community by including all our students in the sharing of the Daily Letter each day. Research suggests that children in the bottom group usually remain in that group throughout elementary school and almost never catch up. We don't want our students to develop the perception that they can't read, as it will likely become self-fulfilling. Be inclusive of all students for the sharing of the Daily Letter component of the literacy program. Pace all students together for the shared reading of the day.

Allington reminds us to have high expectations for all our students. He warns us to resist the tendency to lower expectations for a lower-progress student, but rather to struggle to continue to emphasize full comprehension of text (Allington and Cunningham, 1999).

We want to have students of vastly differing abilities working side-by-side and sharing their Daily Letters with pride. We want to celebrate what each student writes no matter what level that may be.

Your goal is to assist at-risk or low-progress students to feel successful in the large group sharing, by pre-teaching the Daily Letter to them one-to-one or in a small group before the large group sharing of the Daily Letter. Arrange for them to work with it a number of times after the whole group sharing, and at home that night as well. You can be inclusive of all students in the Daily Letter, if some individual teaching of the Daily Letter is given to the most at-risk or low-progress students prior to the whole group Daily Letter sharing.

You don't ever need to make a student perform. Most often your students will lose their fears of oral reading after having the opportunity to practise a script with teacher or tutor. Each success leads to increased self-confidence to motivate repeated success. This is one important purpose for reading.

Ensure that struggling readers are given speaking parts, a situation that reinforces their self-confidence. They should have as many chances to perform as the other students. With the Daily Letter, you can create a situation to reinforce high self-esteem and not limit the performances of at-risk, low-progress students.

9:00	Annie picks up her Daily Letter
9:30	Assistant pre-teaches Daily Letter to Annie
10:45	Annie takes part in the whole-class Daily Letter sharing
12:10	Annie rereads Daily Letter to me at start of lunch
1:00	Annie rereads Daily Letter with Assistant (in class)
2:00	Annie participates in literacy centres
	Annie works with the Daily Letter with her peer tutor
After school	Annie rereads Daily Letter and three old Daily Letters at home with parent

I set aside some time first thing in the morning for my teaching assistant Lynn to pre-teach the Daily Letter to Annie, an at-risk student. Both Lynn and Annie become well versed in the predictable routine of the Daily Letter. Lynn picks up her own copy by the door and quietly slips to the table with Annie to guide Annie's reading of the Daily Letter. She keeps anecdotal comments on her own copy of the Daily Letter as a record of how Annie is doing for my assessment binder.

I want Annie to have 10 to 15 minutes with Lynn to practise the Daily Letter before the whole-class sharing of the it. By the time the Daily Letter sharing happens after recess, Annie will be comfortable with many aspects of the text. This gives Annie a chance to feel included and capable during the whole-group sharing of the Daily Letter.

Sometimes, if there is no one to work with Annie in the early part of the day, I have a former student from a higher grade, well-versed in the Daily Letter strategy, come into the class and review it with her.

Annie needs to spend more time rereading her Daily Letter and needs more support with reading it than other, more able students. Repetition is an important factor for at-risk readers and writers. The difficulty Annie experiences is in direct relationship to the number of repetitions she engages in before reading the text independently. With a predictable routine, Annie has more guided practice using reading and writing strategies. She learns to use the same strategies that other students already use more effectively, the ones I know are just as necessary for Annie to become a better reader and writer.

Annie participates each day with the same Daily Letter that is set out for all the students in the class. Annie's literacy program is not watered down. She will need, however, to spend more time working with the Daily Letter each day in order to master it.

TOP TEN

Tips for Working with At-risk or Low-progress Students

1. accept mistakes, do not criticize them
2. reward small successes; set realistic goals for them
3. make the community a safe classroom for these students—no put downs
4. present good behavior contracts
5. provide immediate rewards and consequences
6. provide conditions that support their ability to concentrate
7. provide daily practice with study and thinking strategies
8. divide tasks up into small parts
9. assign a peer tutor
10. council them on appropriate social behavior

What would happen to your at-risk students if they were able to make a good job of participating with the whole class in the sharing of that day's Daily Letter and again at night with their parents?

Typically some children need to overlearn and internalize language. Literacy educator Margaret Reinhart reminds us that adult standards of boredom do not necessarily apply to children (1990). I notice that many of my students return to their favorite Daily Letters to reread them. Often they turn to the ones they have authored or co-authored to reread. Students continue to enjoy and benefit from reading old favorites. This extended review or practise produces overlearning, reinforces skill, and makes some students feel successful. The Daily Letter may be kept as an anthology of a particular class in the library or as a yearbook for the student.

Support Staff

The Daily Letter can be a convenient means for you or support staff to catch moments here and there out of the busy school day to help at-risk and low-progress students succeed through brief repeated rereading and reviews of the Daily Letter during the day.

Special Education Assistants (SEAs) working with at-risk or low-progress students can work one-on-one or with a small group to assess the progress of students as they participate in the Daily Letter activities. The SEA can report any successes or concerns. They can make brief comments on the Daily Letter and give these to you to add to my assessment and evaluation binder.

I also have the option to review the Daily Letter with the student myself. I may choose to conference with the child alone or in a small group on what was easy or hard. I may want to prepare this student to participate in the next day whole-class Daily Letter sharing.

Cross-class Peer Tutoring

At times, a student from another class can be used to listen to a student repeat reading the Daily Letter. I always look for one of my students from previous years to mentor my most at-risk students. It is kind of a homecoming. These mentors are highly skilled and trained in the teaching of reading from their year with the Daily Letter. They can come to the classroom and work with students for ten minutes, three times a week, and make a significant difference. Rather than organizing my whole class to be with another whole class—which gets really distracting and noisy with 50 students in a classroom—I arrange for one of my old students to quietly slip in and work with one child for ten minutes and then return to his or her regular class. Quite often these special students are willing and able to take ten minutes here and there from their own class and participate in a very important role in mine.

TOP TEN

Conversation Starters for the SEA or Peer Tutor to Ask Student

1. How is it going?
2. Why did you pick this Daily Letter to read?
3. Is the Daily Letter easy, just right, or hard? How do you know?
4. What strategies do you use?
5. Would you read it to me?
6. I was just watching you and I noticed you were _____. Can you tell me about that?
7. Wow! Your reading is really changing! What is different about it?
8. Are you confused about anything?
9. How can I help you?
10. Give it a go.

(adapted from Routman, 1991)

Guided Repeated Oral Reading

Repeated readings with attention to comprehension has been shown to be effective in experimental studies. Here are some tips for teaching guided repeated oral reading to at-risk students:

- Don't have unrehearsed oral reading of the Daily Letter by at-risk students.
- Encourage at-home practice of repeated oral reading of the Daily Letter.
- Practise reading the Daily Letter with teacher guidance and feedback before student reads with the whole class.
- Ensure that the Daily Letter has a balance of successful and challenging words.
- Rehearse until fluent, then perform for the Daily Letter sharing.
- Initially read the text out loud and discuss it with the student.
- Provide support until the student can read it independently with 90% accuracy.
- Don't use oral reading to correct mistakes or tell students unknown words.
- Ensure the support and encouragement of all learners for each oral reading.
- Celebrate the tiny improvements of at-risk students.

Poetry

Some of the best poetry I have seen has come from students who struggle with reading and writing. Poetry is not too long and difficult for some students to attend to. Students can enjoy poetry when they find other forms of writing overwhelming. It can be especially important for students who have English as a second language, as it is a great tool to provide scaffolding of oral language for those apprenticing in English.

TOP TEN

Reasons to Use Poetry with ESL Students

1. Poetry can be short, powerful, and easy to read, and is less intimidating.
2. The rhyme, rhythm, and repetition make poetry easier to decipher for beginning readers and writers.
3. Poetry serves as a brief but powerful anticipatory set for other literature as well as the introduction to concepts and content areas.
4. The variety of poetry formats—such as concrete, found, and model poetry—offer good beginning writing models.
5. Poetry is not graded or leveled.
6. A message comes through in few words.
7. Poems are meant to be read and reread; this promotes fluency.
8. You cover a lot of poetry in a short time; it is a motivating way to spend time reading; and this translates into improved reading in other genres.
9. Readers of poetry are motivated to write poetry.
10. Poetry can be used across the curriculum, in Social Studies, Science, and Math.

What kinds of text do we need to encourage our students to reread? David Booth reminds us that "Poems encourage students to give up their accuracy notion about comprehension and, instead, see the reading of difficult text as a learning process" (1996). At-risk and low-progress readers are asked to read and reread the text, assuming that there will be much that they won't understand the first time or even the second or third time through. Each rereading provides a different kind of understanding of the text and raises new areas of question.

Special Strategies for At-Risk Readers and Writers

We have a number of strategies that provide support for the student who has difficulty with reading and/or for the student who learns through auditory mode. A designated class technician can tape the sharing of the Daily Letter and put the tape into the listening centre for a small group to listen to during literacy centres. One of the students can take it home at the end of the day. This tape can also be kept on hand for further rereadings on other days.

Another strategy we use with at-risk, low-progress students is the use of bookmarks for emergent readers who are not yet skilled in tracking. Students can be trained to use a bookmark to track the Daily Letter text. The teacher can assist any students with the correct method to use it. Students can try holding the bookmark either above or below the text to give students practice with a tool to read fluently.

TOP TEN

Ways to Assist Struggling Readers

1. Read the Daily Letter out loud to the student (this gives ESL students an opportunity to hear the rhythm of the language).
2. Familiarize the student with the text before the shared reading event.
3. Reread text with the student, reading at a pace slightly ahead of his or her speed.
4. Talk about the meaning of the language.
5. Give the student time to reread the text independently.
6. Monitor comprehension through retelling and prediction.
7. Encourage the practice of reading the text publicly with a group to coach the student.
8. During independent reading times, remind the student to use strategies being learned with the Daily Letter.
9. Catch the student doing things right.
10. During centre time, have the student track the story listening to a taped version of the Daily Letter.

Centres

We can use the Daily Letter as a tool to integrate the students' learning from many subject areas. During the afternoon centres, students read, write, and represent their learning in a variety of subject areas, thus dissolving curriculum boundaries. Instead of maintaining blocks of time each day for various separate subject areas, such as Social Studies, Science, Art, Music, and Drama, students can conveniently create/compose Daily Letters on these subjects during literacy centres, covering many of the learning outcomes. The Daily Letter serves as an efficient tool to help students integrate their learning in many areas of the curriculum.

Do you have confident and accurate readers who tend to read their Daily Letter too quickly, with little expression or attention to punctuation? "Practising to perform" gives students a chance to refine their oral reading and emphasize the importance of phrasing and expression for either poetry or other genres.

It is my job to preview the Daily Letters my students make and decide how much support is needed to give to at-risk readers so that they can be at least 90% accurate in their reading of it.

Centring Students in Centres

Centres will run smoothly if they are well organized. Structure them so there is a balance of space, material, groupings, etc. For example, balance the noise level of the classroom by organizing only one centre to be noisy. Have a centre without talking, another where the students whisper as a group, and another where the students whisper in partners.

Another example of a balanced organization of centres would be balancing the use of materials. Plan to have one centre where students use individual pieces of paper to write on, another where students share felt pens and chart paper, another where the students do a reading activity which requires no paper and pencil, and a final centre where the students record their ideas on the chalkboard in large print.

Balance centres considering the following criteria:

Activity Level

> Active vs. settled centres (e.g., role play vs. reading)
> Standing/moving vs. sitting/still centres

Noise Level

> Noisy vs. quiet centres (e.g., drama vs. drawing)
> Working in partners vs. working as individuals

Materials

> Paper-driven vs. activity-oriented centres (e.g., writing in journal vs. building a model out of clay)

Familiarity

> Tried and true/familiar vs. new centres (e.g., reader's theatre that students have participated in many times vs. a Venn diagram that they have never seen before)

Adult Intervention

> Teacher-directed vs. independent

Grouping

> Working alone vs. working in partners, triads, etc.

Accountability

> Individual accountability of the students vs. cooperative accountability

Level of Thinking

> Serious, reflective vs. light/fun centres
> High level vs. low level of thinking/questioning

Task Complexity

> Complicated vs. simple centres
> Complicated (e.g., tasks involving water) vs. simple management of material

Learning Style

> Word smart vs. picture smart vs. body smart
> Interpersonal vs. intrapersonal

Have only one new centre so you don't have to spend too much time explaining how each centre works.

Mini-Daily Letter

The Mini-Daily Letter is a strategy to conduct the Daily Letter as usual but in a small group of four to six students during centre time. Students rotate through four Daily Letters, with the authors of the Daily Letters leading their own and remaining at their own centres.

First, divide the class into four groups, each with an author ready to share his or her Daily Letter with six students. Students sit close together in a group with the author/leader sitting as part of the group. The author takes the group through their Daily Letter in the same way as the Daily Letter is covered with the whole class. The group proceeds with the sharing of the Daily Letter, but in a shortened version, with the literacy event taking no more than 15 to 20 minutes.

The authors/leaders remain in their own quadrants and wait for the next group to rotate to them. The students in each group move, as a group, in a clockwise direction to the next Daily Letter centre. The students move through as many centres as time permits. (One centre = 15 minutes + 5 minutes to rotate to next group.) Two centres would take 40 minutes, three centres would take 60 minutes, and four centres would take 1 hour 20 minutes. Students may be able to do two centres before lunch and two after lunch.

Workshops

If I feel my students do not need the structure of centres—with students in groups moving systematically from centre to centre—I run a workshop.

The students have the choice to read, write, and investigate a wide range of topics for their Daily Letters. They have the time to decide how they want to represent their learning through writing, art, and demonstrations. They are invited to decide for themselves in which mode, style, genre, or medium of expression they wish to explore their thinking on their Daily Letter.

Be available to help students write and talk about their learning, set group/individual goals, reflect with them on their progress, review their Daily Letters, and plan how they will share their learning with the larger community. Post a schedule for students to sign up for conferences with you.

Group 1	Group 2	Group 3	Group 4
Journals	Word Wall	Poetry	Reader's Theatre
Word Wall	Poetry	Reader's Theatre	Journals
Poetry	Reader's Theatre	Journals	Word Wall
Reader's Theatre	Journals	Word Wall	Poetry

Journal Writing Centre: six students sitting at a table at the side of the room

Five students are with me doing some journal writing on a topic of their choice. They sit at the table just beside where I conference each student on his/her writing. I just have enough time to talk to each one of the students. I encourage the students to think about what writing they will want to share on their own Daily Letter at this time.

I keep the option open to have a student remain beside me (even for two or three of the centre rotations) if I feel they need more time writing or are not able to function independently. I invite them to continue to work beside me as a privilege, not as a punishment.

Word Wall: six students standing at the blackboard within easy view

The students at the Word Wall have 15 minutes to construct a list of all the *ar* (car tool) words from their Daily Letters. They construct a list printed large on the blackboard (alone or with a partner from their group) from their search of the pages of today's Daily Letter or past Daily Letters in their binders. They have the option of constructing an *er*, *ir*, or *ur* list of words if they should complete their *ar* word list. At the end of this 15-minute centre the students will share their lists with the whole class before they rotate to their next centre.

Poetry Centre: six students sitting in their own desks in easy view

The students at the poetry centre have 15 minutes to read some Shel Silverstein poetry books from the display case. I ask them to select a poem that they wish to read to the rest of the class at the end of this centre.

Reader's Theatre: six students sitting on the carpet in a circle in easy view

The students have been given a reader's theatre of the *Mr. Bump* story. There are four scripts. They sit on the carpet in a circle and begin the process of selecting who will play which part. The students begin the practising of this funny script. Each student has his or her own copy with his or her lines highlighted in yellow by a parent helper, who has also put the character's name in bold letters on the top.

I have four different *Mr. Men* reader's theatres, so that each group will have a different one to present to the class. By the end of today's centres, each student will have heard three *Mr. Men* reader's theatres besides their own.

One of the secrets of keeping students on task at centres is accountability. By simply having a quick sharing session (5 to 10 minutes) at the end of each centre, the students get in the habit of being prepared to share what they have done, and thus work at harder at it. Focus the attention of the whole class on listening and looking at some of the work the students have done after each centre. Don't wait to do this. Share the reader's theatre performances at this time as yet another read-aloud for your students.

The centres/workshop approach to create Daily Letters is an important method for developing our students' reading, writing, listening, and speaking. It is applicable to all grade levels and subject areas, from early childhood through high school. It features student choice of learning topics, strong teacher modeling, extended student practice, guided goal setting/feedback, and self-directed learning within the story-sharing community. Create a workshop to work closely one-on-one with students while they manage themselves with their own self-directed learning challenges. Students need time to select their own stories/genres so they can interweave knowledge of themselves, each other, and the curriculum together for the entire school year.

CHAPTER 5

Managing the Daily Letter Experience

We can use the Daily Letter as a tool to manage large class numbers with few books and materials. The students and their Daily Letter become the most valuable resource for the teaching of reading, writing, listening, and speaking. Larger classes actually serve to enrich the diverse collection of stories that are crafted and shared with the group. You need nothing but paper and some quality read-alouds, and a workshop with the routine to give students time and space to write on topics of their own choice, to produce a never-ending supply of appealing genres for shared reading and writing. The Daily Letter as a format and routine to teach writing provides an invaluable source of purposeful, appropriate materials and resources for the literacy learning of diverse classes. (See BLM #9 page 75.)

Teaching the Daily Letter

TOP TEN

Things You Should Do when Teaching the Daily Letter

1. avoid rapid fire questions
2. encourage thoughtful reflective answers
3. give students time to share their thinking
4. encourage original answers
5. comment positively on thoughtful responses
6. be genuine
7. ask questions because you really want to know the students' answers
8. encourage students to talk to you by saying such things as, "Go on"
9. watch quietly from the sidelines
10. support and participate to the level required to maximize understanding without dominating the conversation

List of Daily Letters Used in the Elementary Grades

Here are Daily Letters we have used. I'm sure you can come up with even more!

- Short, welcoming Daily Letter paragraph with everyone's name in it
- List of class guidelines generated together just for the class
- Getting Along Songs: Daily Letters for social development
- Schedule of the week: library day, gym day, computer day for students

Checklist for Leader of the Daily Letter

- ❏ Prepare and distribute the Daily Letter to all students.
- ❏ Make sure all the students are prepared: Daily Letter in hand; highlighter ready; colored pencils ready; etc.
- ❏ Make sure overhead is on with transparency of the front page of the Daily Letter showing.
- ❏ Make sure helpers at the overhead are ready and waiting.
- ❏ Introduce yourself.
- ❏ Introduce the title and genre of the Daily Letter.
- ❏ Establish the purpose for reading; for example, are you reading for enjoyment, or skimming?
- ❏ Give a summary statement of the Daily Letter in two or three sentences.
- ❏ Ask the students what they already know about the topic.
- ❏ "Walk" through the text by looking briefly at it.
- ❏ Discuss any special aspects of the letter-size page.
- ❏ Review the vocabulary you think students may need help with.
- ❏ Make sure everyone can see and hear everyone else; remind the students to stand when speaking.
- ❏ Share each component of the Daily Letter.
- ❏ Compliment (being specific) or thank students for taking part in the Daily Letter conversation.

- A biography of the principal, vice-principal, librarian of the school
- A Blessed Book list with every child in the class and his or her favorite book listed: bring tents and camp for the day, reading favorite books
- Daily Letters about favorite colors/color poems
- A Thanks A Lot Song for the Daily Letter: things we are thankful for
- Information and reflections on daily activities in the classroom
- Celebrations: e.g., class Halloween party invitation, Halloween Daily Letters, a story and graph of Halloween candies
- A letter of congratulations to go with contributions to a charity; e.g., the Terry Fox Foundation
- A list of instructions; e.g., chocolate pudding fingerpainting
- Expert personal narrative: rock hounds, gymnasts, ballet dancers, pianists, painters
- An invitation to a guest author
- A memoir; e.g., a student's Grandpa who is a war hero
- A description of the class pet tarantula and spider research
- Dialogues; e.g., between the students and a Halloween skeleton hanging on the wall
- A know/wonder learn chart; e.g., on bog mummies
- An excerpt from Friendship books
- Christmas Around the World
- Class New Year's resolutions
- Reader's theatre scripts: commercial or student-made
- Advertisement; e.g., kittens for sale by a student in the class
- Autobiographies of class members, birthday Daily Letters
- Bibliography; e.g., books by Shel Silverstein
- An article for the school newspaper; e.g., on the running of our recycling program
- Cartoons drawn by a class member; e.g., learning styles information for parents
- Instructions; e.g., for play clay art, from the Barbara Reid book *Effie*
- A character sketch; e.g., of Mario from Super Mario Brothers
- Author study
- Pizza Day menu
- Summaries of the class's Science Fair projects
- People in the community
- Jokes and riddles
- Reflection on Career Day highlights
- A class list; e.g., for Valentine cards
- Student's choice of fiction and non-fiction
- Directions; e.g., for origami fortune tellers
- Reader responses on favorite chapter books
- Lists of observations; e.g., of the owl who visited the classroom
- Family trees, stories, and histories
- Research on family treasures, to be shared in a Family Treasure Exhibit
- Field trip summaries, learning logs, reflections
- A coded message by a student
- List of Sports Day events
- Growing instructions for plants
- Learning logs; e.g., on provinces in Canada, Painted Lady butterflies
- Dr. Seuss goodbye story for year-end

The Daily Letter at Different Grade Levels

We have different routines and formats for Daily Letters in early primary and late primary/intermediate. There will be a wide variety of differences in the language, ideas, and organization, the graphics and the format of the Daily Letter from grade to grade, class to class. There are, however, some general characteristics of reading material that is suitable for most of the students in each grade. As teachers, we need to learn what materials our students can reasonably expected to read with understanding in our classes.

The great beauty of the Daily Letter is that you can monitor and adjust the characteristics and topics of it to suit the literacy learning interests and needs of your students. Teachers of students from Grade 1 to Grade 7 are realizing excellent results in classroom with their own personalized versions of the Daily Letter. The Daily Letter format is flexible enough to be used effectively with students in public or private schools, special programs, and home schooling settings.

The Early Primary Daily Letter

Many Kindergarten, Grade 1, and Grade 2 teachers find the Daily Letter an invaluable resource of easy-to-produce text at a level that matches the students when they arrive at school on the first day. It is a practical, efficient way to personalize reading material for groups of emergent readers and writers. See BLMs #10 page 81, #11 page 82 and #11A page 83, #12 page 84 and #12A page 85 for templates.

Routines

Grade 1 students can "read" on the first day of school when their teacher composes a special Daily Letter for and about them, often composed of about three to six beginning words.

Our goal with students in the early primary grades is to develop positive attitudes towards reading and writing with our sharing of the Daily Letter. You will want to make your first routine shared-language experiences short and sweet. Put the Daily Letter on a large chart, and gather the students close to read together. Use a pointer to track the story and the short word list on the bottom of the chart. Eventually the students will read the Daily Letter from their own pages.

You may need to take months to model reading and writing on the Daily Letters you have constructed. Teach the conventions of print, spelling, printing and punctuation on the Daily Letters you share with your students. Over time, the modeling, coding, and strategic teaching will begin to transfer into the students' writing and reading practice. Then, you can begin to publish their Daily Letters.

It may be quite late in the year before you publish students' work on the Daily Letter. First encourage young writers to write in what ever way they are able. Students in Grade 1 will get to the point where they can go through the process of prewriting, drafting, and sharing their own Daily Letters.

Spend lots of time on prewriting about experiences you have had first-hand together. Closely guide students' writing process by modeling the writing of these Daily Letter stories on a large chart with them. Do lots of brainstorming of words, and making easy-to-see lists to help writers see the various aspects of text they will want to use. Your goal with these students is not to focus on only conventions such as spelling, printing, and punctuation, even though that is what you do most often on teacher-made Daily Letters. Don't worry about correctness in their writing yet. Fluency is more important. Over time, you can shape their approximations of text to look more like that of conventional adult text. It will take time. You need to keep doing Daily Letters with them and give them this time to learn about literacy in the safety of the story-sharing community.

Here are some considerations of sharing the Daily Letter with early primary students:

- Daily Letter language experience should be of short duration: 15 to 20 minutes
- word study of four to eight words (20 to 40 per week)
- make the print for emergent readers large, clear, and double-spaced
- make sure the Daily Letter is not too hard for the majority of the students
- pre-teach the Daily Letter to students who are not able to read the Daily Letter with 90% accuracy
- begin with a simple, non-threatening format that takes up one side of a letter-size page
- keep sight of the goal of developing a positive attitude towards reading and writing
- work the coding of the text as an active, social, engaging method to learn concepts of writing
- share with your students the goal to develop reading and writing fluency
- give your students knowledge of the purpose of writing
- the Daily Letter may remain a primarily teacher-directed language experience with very young students
- use a simplified writing process: prewriting, drafting, and sharing
- write Daily Letters together as shared writing by the whole class
- get lots of help from adults to work with individual writers/readers
- systematically add sight words, basic spelling patterns to the Daily Letter each day
- demonstrate mechanics such as spelling, printing, and punctuation
- have students do lots of writing and drawing, or drawing and writing
- accept the students' approximations of text as a first stage of becoming writers
- as the year progresses, increase the difficulty of the text and time spent exploring the Daily Letter (see page 86)
- increase the amount of talk about text by the students
- educate the parents of your students about invented spelling and approximations of print; explain the writing/reading process for emergent writers/readers
- have students learn phonemic awareness through the addition of a word study on the back of he Daily Letter part way through the year
- encourage students to read their Daily Letter to each of their family members each night

Format

The general characteristics of the language, ideas, organization, graphics, and format of early primary Daily Letters are simple and repetitive. The ideas are generally close to the students' own experiences in the classroom. Use lots of illustrations to support the written text, which is linear with large, simple, clear print. There should be lots of empty space on the Daily Letter.

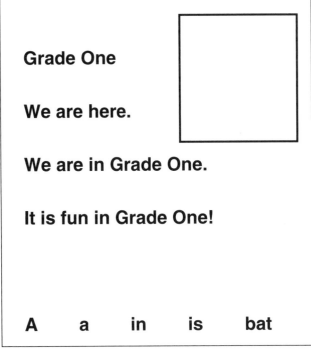

Grade One

We are here.

We are in Grade One.

It is fun in Grade One!

A   a   in   is   bat

Front

(There is no back to the Daily Letter for the first months of Grade 1. Students are not ready to participate in the reading and writing activities placed here.)

Back

The early primary Daily Letter has the following characteristics:

Format

- Wide space between words
- Linear text
- Early in Grade 1, typically three to ten sentences
- Early in Grade 1, typically three to ten lines of information
- Short sentences, may continue down to next line
- Large amount of blank space on the page

Ideas and Organization

- Close to experiences of students
- Imaginative stories
- Home–adventure–home stories
- Predictable characters
- Clear sequence of events
- Humor
- Information material is short with illustrations to convey much of the information

Language

- Simple
- Repetitive
- Lots of high-frequency words
- Lots of shape, size, color, number words
- New words that are easy to decode
- New words that are easy to understand
- Special words supported with illustrations
- No change in verb tense

- A few sentence patterns
- Poetry with repetition, rhythm, rhyme
- Words in poetry with interesting sounds
- Simple dialogue

Graphics

- Support the text
- Increasing amount of space is given to the text
- Information conveyed through the picture

TOP TEN

Choices of Personalized Reading Material for Early Primary Daily Letters

1. Reflections on our day: Today we…, we are…, or we have…
2. News of our day
3. Introductions to our VIPs; i.e., our class
4. Retellings of patterned stories related to our lives
5. Retellings of rebus stories related to our lives
6. Personal stories: tooth fairy, family, pet, birthday, and scar stories
7. Stories and pictures of our school spirit events: Sports Day, Pajama Day, Hat Day, field trips, etc.
8. Being heard as experts: rock hounds, gymnasts, ballerinas, scientists, etc.
9. Important people in our lives: family members, guests
10. Sharing the personal lives of teachers and other adults, such as principal, vice-principal, librarian, etc.

The Late Primary/Intermediate Daily Letter

Routines

Teachers in the late primary years and the intermediate grades have a "bite-size" piece of text to work with each day to fit it all in, to teach an ever-expanding curriculum to an increasingly diverse range of learners. Teachers of late primary and intermediate classes can use the Daily Letter as a tool to teach across the curriculum. Students in these grades can share the responsibility with the teacher for the teaching/learning of the Daily Letter for up to an hour each day. They can each be groomed for a student-as-teacher leadership role to share a Daily Letter and disperse growing literacy understandings and skills with the other member of the story-writing community. See BLMs #13 page 89 and #13A page 90 for template.

You can have in-depth coverage of a wide variety of subject/curriculum areas with late primary and intermediate students leading the Daily Letter. You can provide each student with a number of important opportunities as self-directed learners and leaders. Teachers in these grades may find this multi-purpose teaching tool indispensable for challenging their diverse groups of students to write in many genres, from personal narrative to expository text. It is important to keep in mind that the gap between more able and less able writers widens as the students get older. This method of sharing many strategies through one page of text is useful to teach a variety of abilities. It is a particularly useful tool for teaching late-blooming literacy learners.

Beginning Grade 1 Daily Letter Template

Grade 1 Daily Letter   Date: _____

Author: _____   Genre: _____

_____   _____   _____   _____   _____   _____

Ask me to . . . _____.

Mid-year Grade 1 Daily Letter Template: Front

Grade 1 Daily Letter   **Date:** _____

Author: _____   **Genre:** _____

_____   _____   _____   _____   _____   _____

Ask me to . . . _____.

Mid-year Grade 1 Daily Letter Template: Back

I/we have shared the Daily Letter together: _____ **signature**

Messages and Compliments:

_____

_____

Poem, Song, or Chant

End of Year Grade 1 Daily Letter Template: Front

Author: _____   **Genre:** _____

Title: _____

Word Study: _____   _____   _____

_____   _____   _____   _____

Ask me about _____ .

End of Year Grade 1 Daily Letter Template: Back

I/We have listened to my/our child share their Daily Letter. Comments:

_____

_____ Signature:_____

Word Study: **Song, Chant or Rhyme**

_____

_____

_____

_____

_____

_____

_____

_____

Retell, Relate, Reflect

_____

_____

_____

_____

The train was filled with other children, all in their pajamas and nightgowns. We sang Christmas carols and ate candies with nougat centers as white as snow. We drank hot cocoa as thick and rich as melted chocolate bars. Outside, the lights of towns and villages flickered in the distance as the Polar Express raced northward.

Soon there were no more lights to be seen. We traveled through cold, dark forests, where lean wolves roamed and white-tailed rabbits hid from our train as it thundered through quiet wilderness.

We climbed mountains so high it seemed as if we would scrape the moon. But the Polar Express never slowed down. Faster and faster we ran along, rolling over peaks and through valleys like a car on a roller coaster (Van Allsburg, 1985).

chocolate Christmas   climbed timed   tails trains mountains   coasters cocoa roamed highlights white   through true blue

??? Ask me about the first gift of Christmas.   ???

Front

Word Study:

Whatif
Last night as I lay thinking here,
Some Whatifs crawled inside my ear
And pranced and partied all night long
And sang their same old Whatif song:
Whatif I'm dumb in school?
Whatif they closed the swimming pool?
Whatif I get beat up?
Whatif there's poison in my cup?
Whatif I start to cry?
Whatif I get sick and die?
Whatif I flunk the test?
Whatif green hair grows on my chest?
Whatif nobody likes me?
Whatif a bolt of lightening strikes me?
Whatif I don't grow taller?
Whatif my head starts getting smaller?
Whatif fish won't bite?
Whatif wind tears up my kite?
Whatif they start a war?
Whatif my parents get divorced?
Whatif the bus is late?
Whatif my teeth don't grow in straight?
Whatif I tear my pants?
What if I never learn to dance?
Everything seems swell, and then
The nighttime Whatifs strike again!
Shel Silverstein

Back

Here are some considerations of sharing the Daily Letter with late primary/intermediate students:

- increase the duration of Daily Letter language experience over the course of the year from 40 minutes to 70 minutes
- word study consists of 8 to 12 words (40 to 60 words per week)
- increase the difficulty of the Daily Letter over the course of the year
- work more difficult text through more coding of the text
- ensure the full inclusion of all students in the talk about the text of the Daily Letter
- share with the students the goals of developing positive attitude towards writing and reading, public speaking
- develop concepts, skills, and attitudes of all writers
- increase the number and variety of formal genres on the Daily Letter
- notice that the writing may become less situated in the lives of the students
- strive for the inclusion of proper conventions of print, spelling, and punctuation
- strive to give students the knowledge of number of purposes/functions of writing
- use the full professional format of process writing: prewriting, drafting, editing, proofreading, publishing
- increase the number of lead roles of your student authors
- strive to have the students be self-directed in their learning
- increase students' independence from the teacher and other adults
- have peers conferencing individual writers
- bathe your student in word studies of lists of key words, origins of words, subject words, interesting and unusual words

- insist that published formats come close to conventional adult forms
- invite students to present more complex Daily Letter literacy events
- invite students to collaborate to produce unique, original Daily Letters
- make the students completely responsible for organizing and teaching Daily Letter language experiences
- include lots of opportunities for self-assessment of the literacy learning of the story-sharing community

Format

The late primary/intermediate Daily Letter has the following characteristics:

Format

- Standard word spacing
- Decreasing from 14- to 12-point font over the intermediate years
- Text becomes a block with space at the bottom of the page
- Graphics become more complex sources of information
- Mostly linear text
- Typically more than five to ten sentences
- Typically more than five to ten bits of information
- Variety of lengths of sentences, many will continue down to next line
- Fewer illustrations with stories
- Less to little space on the page

Ideas and Organization

- Topics not so close to experiences of students but generally about characters their own age
- Themes of friendship, growing up
- Increasing complexity of characters
- Characters are revealed rather than described
- Increasing amount of description
- Setting, mood of the story become more important
- Solutions to problems may be surprising
- Element of suspense
- Paragraphs of varied length
- Stories have a moral or a message
- Poetry has more abstract concepts and description
- Imaginative stories with lots of action
- Some twists in plots of the story
- Humor
- Information material is longer with text and illustrations both conveying information

Language

- Straightforward
- Conversation
- Use of more interesting, unusual, or challenging words
- Longer amounts of narration
- More descriptive language
- Poetry includes figurative language
- Some free verse

- Special words may not be supported with illustrations
- Wider variety of sentence lengths with more complex sentence structure
- A few different sentence patterns
- Poetry has repetition, rhythm, rhyme
- Words in poetry have interesting sounds
- Simple dialogue

Graphics

- Support, enhance the text
- Increasing amount of space is given to the text

TOP TEN

Topics of Daily Letters in the Intermediate Grades

1. Reflections of our day
2. Non-fiction reflective research: Why and How questions of students' choice
3. Fiction of students' choice
4. Biographies of our community, autobiographies
5. Scientist of the week: selected and prepared by students
6. Learning logs, journals
7. Retellings of our stories: family histories and family treasures
8. Personal narrative: family stories, pet and scar stories
9. News of our week: school spirit events, etc.,
10. Persuasive writing: critical examination of book, author, articles, essays, advertisements

Late Primary or Intermediate Daily Letter Template: Front

AUTHOR: **GENRE:**

WORD STUDY:

ASK ME...

Late Primary or Intermediate Daily Letter Template: Back

I/we have shared the Daily Letter together: _____ signature

Messages and Compliments:

_____

_____

Word Study: Song, Poem, or Chant

_____

_____

_____

_____

_____

_____

_____

_____

_____

_____

Retell, Relate, Reflect

_____

_____

_____

_____

CHAPTER 6

Strategy Instruction

We want to cultivate reflection.... The way that we do this is by immersing students in talk—talk about their experiences, talk about their ideas, talk about words—for it is through talk that we develop the ability to reflect.... We wrap talk in, through and around experiences to help them develop the ability to reflect in action, *and we talk afterward (debrief) to develop the ability to* reflect on action. *(Chapman, 1997)*

There are many thinking strategies that support and guide a student to process written language. A reader needs to become consciously aware of these strategies, to become an alert, strategic problem solver making effective choices to process text. These strategies are not formulas, but options to help a learner construct meaning. We want all our students to become familiar with a variety and number of strategies that are used by successful readers and writers. We want then to begin to understand what happens within the reading and writing processes.

You can effectively model what good readers, writers, listeners, and thinkers do each day with a small amount of Daily Letter text. Using small amounts of text on the Daily Letter is beneficial to all students, but especially at-risk students who cannot handle large amounts of print and yet are in need of more practice with strategies than other students are. Support students in the repeated use of strategies with each Daily Letter to constantly orient them to become increasingly more independent, strategic thinkers.

It would be nice to think that students acquired the strategies and skills they need to be successful readers and writers without explicit instruction; however, both research and classroom experience suggest that there are times when modeling, scaffolding, and strategic teaching benefit a child. Eventually, they will need to become responsible for their own independent use of strategies—but not just yet. Some of the most at-risk students will need to work with strategies many, many times to internalize how to use them independently. Monitor your students as they learn to apply them on their own in different settings. Later in the year you can extend the amount of time given to the independent use of strategies with materials of greater length for more capable students.

Much of the time spent on the Daily Letter is devoted to improving the use of thinking strategies of readers and writers. The majority of the strategy teaching is done with the whole group sharing the Daily Letter. The talk-alouds on each of the components last up to ten minutes. Observe how children use their strategies during the Daily Letter. This information can be used to plan for individual and small-group lessons on strategies. Much of this teaching will be done one-to-one or in small groups in the afternoon centres. Sometimes, at-risk students may have the opportunity to review with the learning assistant some of the strategies good readers and writers use, before they participate in the whole-group teaching of the Daily Letter. If you see that a student needs more work with learning and using a particular strategy, you can decide then the best time to reteach it.

Using Think-aloud Strategies

You can transform your classroom into a story-sharing community by demonstrating what, why, how, and when to use each thinking strategy with students.

- What: Identify the strategy to be taught.
- Why: Tell why it is to be used.
- How: Tell how you use the strategy, in steps.
    Model the use of the strategy during the Daily Letter sharing.
- What: List the strategy on a chart in plain view for easy reference for the readers and writers.
- When: Encourage students to adapt the strategy for independent use.
    Continue to monitor the students' independent use of the strategy.

The sharing of the think-aloud strategies of the Daily Letter is part of a rigorous, recurrent, specific, and tightly organized literacy event. It requires considerable time and skill to implement properly. It demands more management on the part of the teacher and more discipline from the students than traditional methods of literacy learning. It requires that teacher, students, and parents participate in a wide variety and number of leading, teaching, and talking roles throughout the school year to move from apprenticing to instructing/mentoring roles.

See BLMs #14 page 93, #15 page 94 and #15A page 95, to see the think-aloud strategies used for each component of the Daily Letter.

See BLMs #14 page 93, #15 page 94 and #15A page 95

Strategies for Using the Front of the Daily Letter

Author Share

The author/leader of the Daily Letter introduces him- or herself and talks briefly about one aspect of the writing process he or she went through. The author/leader describes what he or she had to think about as an author while writing this genre.

Strategy at a Glance

What: Introduce the Author Share strategy.
Why: Introduce the strategy as a way to become a better writer.
How: • Share one part of your act of writing of the Daily Letter being shared.
    • Talk briefly about what you were thinking when you wrote it.
What: • Record this on the What Good Writers Do chart. Remind the students to use the strategy independently.

Think-alouds for Author Share Strategies

- Good writers discover their subject; they select topics they know/care about.
- Good writers find the right voice for their composition.

What Good Writers Do chart

1. Good writers search for specifics.
2. Good writers speak with a voice of authority.
3. Good writers introduce use their own life experiences for ideas.
4. Good writers start with action.
5. Good writers do research.
6. Good writers use leads that hook the reader.
7. Good readers know their audience.
8. Good writers write about things they know about.
9. Good writers make pictures in the reader's minds.
10. Good writers show not tell.
11. Good writers make their ideas flow.
12. Good writers use quotation marks to show the reader when a person is talking in the story.
13. Good writers don't finish every story.

BLM #14

Checklist of Think-Aloud Strategies by Component

Component	Strategies
1. Author, Title, Genre	❏ Author Share
	❏ Analogies Between Texts
2. Text	❏ Activating Prior Knowledge
	❏ Reading: Pupil Partner Read
	❏ Reading: Radio Read
	❏ Reading: Silent Support
	❏ Coding the Text
	❏ Building the Word Wall
3. Graphics	❏ Visualization
	❏ Visual Artist Share
4. Reading Word Study	❏ Say It Fast!
5. Ask Me Prompt	❏ 30-second Talk
6. Comments/Compliments	❏ Three Stars and a Wish
7. Writing Word Study	❏ See It, Say It, Check It
8. Poetry, Song or Chant	❏ Poet Share
	❏ Choral Reading
9. Written Response/Reflection	❏ Recall, Relate, and Reflect
10. Wild Card: choice component	❏ Think-aloud about the choice component

Components of the Daily Letter and Strategies: Front

1. Author: _____   Genre:_____
    Strategy: Author Share   **Strategy: Analogies Between Texts**

    Title: _____

2. Text
    Strategy: Activating Prior Knowledge
    Strategy: Pupil Partner Read
    Strategy: Coding the Text
    Strategy: Building the Word Wall

                                    3. Graphics
                                        Strategy: Visualization
                                        Strategy: Visual Artist Share

4. Reading Word Study
    Strategy: Say It Fast

    _____   _____   _____   _____

5. Ask Me what I learned about…
    Strategy: 30-second Talk

BLM #15A

Components of the Daily Letter and Strategies: Back

We/I have reviewed the Daily Letter: _____ (initials)

6. Comments:
   Strategy: Three Stars and A Wish

7. Writing Word Study
   Strategy: See it, Say it, Check It

8. Poetry, Chants, Songs
   Strategy: Poet Share
   Strategy: Choral Reading

9. Written Response
   Strategy: Recall, Relate, Reflect

10. Wild Card ???
    Strategy: Think-aloud

- Good writers design the presentation of their letters/words carefully.
- Good writers choose the names of their characters carefully.
- Good writers appeal to the senses, particularly the sense of smell.
- Good writers create pictures in a reader's mind; they show not tell.
- Good writers use conventions of print to help the reader read the story clearly.
- Good writers think about what will be clear, be powerful, and make sense to a particular audience.
- Good writers focus, focus, focus.
- Good writers make a powerful beginning to their text (i.e., use action).
- Good writers think of a title that will hook the reader.
- Good writers think about a title after they have written the story.
- Good writers put lots of information in, and write with a voice of authority.
- Good writers edit their writing.
- Good writers read their work to other people to see if it makes sense.
- Good writers use their own ideas and sometimes they use the ideas of others.
- Good writers talk to other writers.

Analogies Between Texts

The author/leader of the Daily Letter introduces the genre to the class and briefly talks about how and why the format was selected. The author/leader can ask students to make connections to previous genres they have read and talked about on the Daily Letter.

Strategy at a Glance

What: Introduce the Analogies Between Texts strategy.

Why: Introduce this strategy as a way to become a better writer and have a better understanding of text.

How: • Have the students skim the text of the Daily Letter being shared.
- Share one similarity and one difference between this Daily Letter format and a previous day's Daily Letter format.
- Talk briefly about what you know about the two genres: What is similar? What is different? What do you notice about the way this genre is presented? Are there any clues as to how the reader/writer works with this genre?

What: • List this genre on the Genres We Know chart.

Think-alouds for Analogies Between Texts

- A person who shares a form of writing that is clear to the reader is a good writer.
- Good writers use their imagination to write some genres.
- Good writers think about the most supportive format for what they want to say.
- Good writers control the format of the text to suit their communication needs.
- Good writers don't have every part of their genre figured out when they begin.

Genres We Know chart

1. personal narrative
2. expository text
3. description
4. persuasive writing
5. combined information text/ narrative
6. eulogy
7. poetry
8. songs
9. chants
10. e-mail
11. newspaper article

Book Pick for more information on
Genre:
Weaving Webs of Meaning by Marilyn
Chapman

TOP TEN

Topics for Genre-sharing Strategies

 1. what you notice about the genre
 2. comparing genres
 3. contrasting genres
 4. what genre it is by the format; characteristics
 5. function of the genre in the world
 6. why this genre works
 7. classification of the genre as formal or informal
 8. classification of the genre as spoken or written genre
 9. the genre is useful to whom?
10. evidence of several genres

Activating Prior Knowledge

The author/leader of the Daily Letter introduces the topic of the Daily Letter and asks the story-sharing community what they already know about the topic. The group can list or brainstorm what they know about the topic.

Strategy at a Glance

What: Introduce the Activating Prior Knowledge Pre-reading strategy.
Why: Introduce this strategy as a way to become a better reader.
How: • Ask the students to talk briefly about what they already know about the topic of the text. Share everything they know about it.
  • Ask them to listen as they read for things they did not know about the topic.

Think-alouds for Accessing Prior Knowledge

- Good readers think about the topic and think about what they already know about it before they read it.
- Good readers preview a text by skimming through it.
- Good readers ask questions before they read a text.
- Good readers think about the title of the reading material before reading it.
- Good readers make personal connections before reading new text.
- Good readers visualize what the story is about before reading it.

Reading

Think-alouds for Reading

- Good readers self-correct, read ahead, and reread.
- Good readers adjust their reading rate.
- Good readers ask, "Does it make sense?" They think about the illustrations, the story structure, and what they know about what they are reading to make sense of it.
- Good readers ask, "Does it sound right?" They listen for natural language.
- Good readers ask, "Does it look right? Does it match the print?" They look at the beginning, middle, and end letters and their corresponding sounds as one way to read a word.

- Good readers look at the words before and after an unknown word, the punctuation, and other conventions of print.
- Good readers visualize what the author is saying.
- Good readers verify any predictions they have made.
- Good readers discuss code or take notes to understand difficult text.

Pupil Partner Read

In this strategy (Whistler, 1976), the author/leader of the Daily Letter asks the students to take turns read the Daily Letter in partners, talking about the strategies they use to decode words.

Strategy at a Glance

What: Introduce the Pupil Partner Read strategy.
Why: Tell the students this will help them become better readers.
How: • Have students decide on partners.
- Have one partner read half the text with the other partner listening to how the reader figures out words they do not know.
- Have the person listening cue their partner if they are stuck on a word.
    Does it look right?
    Does it sound right?
    Does it make sense?
- Switch roles for reading the second half of the text.
- Have the partners talk about strategies they use to solve words.
- Review several of the reading strategies students use with the larger story-sharing community.

TOP TEN

Things Good Readers Do

1. Set a purpose for reading
2. Skim titles and headings.
3. Skim pictures, photographs, and graphics.
4. Use visualization to understand reading.
5. Use words around the words (context clues) to figure out hard words.
6. Predict and confirm the predictions.
7. Ask questions, and read or reread to understand what is read.
8. Make connections to the text.
9. Ask for help if they need it.
10. Make inferences.

Radio Reading

This strategy (Vacca & Vacca, 1989) is designed to have students listen to language, to focus on the meaning without looking at the text.

Strategy at a Glance

What: Introduce the Radio Reading strategy
Why: Tell the students this will help them become better listeners.

How: • Tell a students to close his or her book and listen to the Daily Letter without looking at it.
      • Have the student listen to the Daily Letter with the texts in front of him or her.
When: • Review this reading strategy with the larger story-sharing community from time to time.

Silent Support

The author/leader of the Daily Letter engages the students in improving their reading of the text with this strategy. This strategy is designed to have students support each other in pairs as they read the Daily Letter.

Strategy at a Glance

What: Introduce the Silent Support strategy
Why: Tell the students this will help them become better readers
How: • Have students decide on partners.
      • Tell the students they are to read their books quietly.
      • Either student can ask for help as they read the text.

TOP TEN

Strategies Used by Good Readers

1. predicting what will happen next
2. accessing previous experiences, knowledge, feelings ("Think of a time when…")
3. making pictures in your mind
4. rereading, slowing down, reading ahead, skipping and coming back
5. making it make sense
6. reading the punctuation
7. reading the visuals, graphics
8. monitoring comprehension
9. asking another reader for help
10. scanning the text to look for specific information

Coding the Text

Book Pick for more information on Reading Strategies:
An Observation Survey of Early Literacy Achievement by Marie M. Clay

The author/leader of the Daily Letter engages the students in talk about the text by providing prompts for the students, such as finding a word, phrase, or sentence in the story that is easy, is hard, has a personal connection, etc. The students search through the text to find suitable responses to the prompt, highlight them, and share them with the story-sharing community. See BLMs #16 page 100 for prompts for coding, and #17 page 102 for coding tools.

Think-alouds for Coding

• Good writers need to be able to think about how words look, including the clusters and patterns in the words (phonemic strategies).
• Good writers learn how words sound and the relationship between letters and clusters (visual strategies).

STRETCH Prompt Chart

Strategic Teaching Reaching Everyone—Teaching Children How to…

Choose some of these prompts to use with your students

Code and talk about conventions of print, letters, and words:

- an upper case letter (capital), a lower case letter (small); favorite letter, name initial
- bold face, italics; a punctuation mark (. , ! ? # @ $ ^& ( ) [ ] \ " ")
- indented text, a space, a mistake

Code and talk about a word, phrase, or sentence you can respond to:

- something interesting, you like, you don't like, you would like to share
- something you do not understand (confuses you), you don't agree with, is a problem
- something that makes you laugh or cry, or think; you will think about again
- something that makes you think of a special food, color, time, or person
- something that is real, is not real
- something you have a question about, you could draw, you couldn't draw
- something you would like to remember or find out more about
- something that tells what the story is about, the main idea, a detail
- something that is like another word you know, has a word in it
- something that that could happen to you, is important to you, you can say in your own words

Code and talk about words or letters that have special sounds:

- have consonants or vowels that are the good guys; they talk
- have consonants or vowels that are the tough guys; they don't talk
- rhyme, end in the same sound, begin with the same sound
- have a little word in the bigger word (neat – eat, pink – ink, soften – often)
- you can add a letter to, or mix the letters up to make a new word
- a letter that is tall, short; with circles, tunnels, a tail, a dot, a cross; you see often
- favorite letter or word, least favorite letter or word
- a sound that different pairs or sets of letters make: ch, sh, th , wh, st, sp, sn, sm, sl, sc, sk, sw, bl, cl, fl, gl, pl, br, cr, dr, fr, pr, tr; spl, str, spr, scr, squ; ar, or, er, ir , ur; ou, ow, oo, oi, oy; nk, ck, ke; dge, ge, tch, ch; tion, ture; ic, le; igh, ight
- are small, medium, or large; have 2, 3, 4, 5, 6, 7, 8, or more letters or syllables
- synonyms, antonyms, homonyms, abbreviations, contractions, compounds
- have a prefix, suffix, root word
- a simile, a metaphor

Code and talk about a word, phrase or sentence you can think about that

- you knew right away, you guessed, was tricky to solve, you didn't get
- you had to look at the words around it to figure it out
- had a part that gives a clear and vivid picture in your mind
- you had to break apart and put back together in order to read it

- Good writers know how words represent meaning through combinations of word parts (morphemic strategies).
- Good writers know that similar words can be used to figure out unfamiliar words through making analogies between word (connecting strategies).
- Good writers use materials, references, and resources to understand words (inquiry strategies).

Strategy at a Glance

What: Introduce the Coding the Text strategy.

Why: Introduce the strategy as a way to become better readers and writers.

How: • Introduce the STRETCH chart selected for that day's Daily Letter.
- Select a prompt from the STRETCH chart and have the students look for answers to the prompt in the text of the Daily Letter.
- Have volunteers share their ideas related to the prompt.
- Have each student talk to the other students about why they made the selection they did from the text.
- Have everyone highlight these selected conventions, words, or sentences.
- Talk briefly about what you understand about today's text.

Words	Symbol
Liked	+ or ++
Disliked	- or —
Unknown	?
Hero	**
Can touch	F
Can't touch	×
Person	highlight in yellow

Building the Word Wall

As the story-sharing community participates in the coding of the text with the leader of the Daily Letter, the teacher can add new words to the Word Wall.

Strategy at a Glance

What: Introduce the Building the Word Wall strategy.

Why: Introduce the strategy as a way for students to be better spellers, writers, and readers.

How: • Listen as students find words in the text to answer the STRETCH chart prompts during the Coding of Text strategy.
- Have students decide which column of the Word Wall to place the word being coded on the Daily Letter.

What: • List the words they are coding on the Word Wall.

When: • Encourage students to use the Word Wall independently as a tool for their own writing.
- Encourage students to ask you to add words from other sources (independent novel reading, reader's theatre) to the Word Wall during other parts of the school day.

TOP TEN

Reading Strategies

1. figuring out unknown words
2. reading words carefully
3. recognizing words quickly
4. checking to see if a word looks right
5. using the strategies that good readers do
6. noticing word parts, syllables
7. locating answers on the page, in your head, or on the page and in your head

Tools to Use When Coding the Daily Letter

Chart	Tool	Placement
words with *a*		draw apple above *a* in *can*
words with *le*		draw table above *le* in *fable*
words with *ake*		draw a cake above the *ake* in *make*
words with *ai*		draw a nail above the *ai* in *gain*
words with *all*		draw a ball above the *all* in *tall*
words with *ay*		draw a crayon above the *ay* in *pay*
words with *au*		draw an auto above the *au* in *August*
words with *aw*		draw a saw above the *aw* in *claw*
words with *ar*		draw a star above the *ar* in *yard*
words with *oo*		draw a book above the *oo* in *took*
words with *oo*		draw a broom above the *oo* in *zoom*
words with *ck*		draw a block above the *ck* in *black*
words with *c*		draw a cat above the *c* in *camp*
words with *c*		draw a city above the *c* in *centre*
words with *ch*		draw a chair above the *ch* in *chain*
words with *cl*		draw a clock above the *cl* in *clamp*
words with *cr*		draw a crab above the *cr* in *crazy*
words with *dr*		draw a drum above the *dr* in *drop*
words with *ee*		draw a deer above the *ee* in *steer*
words with *ea*		draw a peach above the *ea* in *flea*
words with *ate*		draw a gate above the *ate* in *plate*

8. putting words together so they sound like talking
9. checking to see if a word looks right
10. not knowing every word

Visualization of Text

The leader of the Daily Letter has the students visualize one aspect of the text and draw it in the text box.

Strategy at a Glance

What: Introduce the Visualization strategy

Why: Introduce this strategy as a way to help students understand a text.

How: • Have everyone read and make a mental image of what the author is saying.
  • Have them draw a picture on the front of the Daily Letter.
  • Share their pictures with others.

Visualization Artist Share

During text instruction, the leader of the Daily Letter has the students examine/discuss in detail the tables, charts, graphs, etc., to assist them in clarifying concepts that are discussed in the text. The leader also shares one aspect of the process of creating the visual.

Strategy at a Glance

What: Introduce the Visual Artist Share strategy.

Why: Introduce this strategy as a way to understand the text and become a better visual artist.

How: • Show the student graphics that are integrated with the texts on the Daily Letter.
  • Show the key features of the graphics and explain the steps in making them.

When: • Challenge students to represent some of their learning on future Daily Letters in visual form.

Think-alouds for Visualization

- Good illustrators need to make clear, concise visual information to appropriately support the written text.
- Good illustrators need to focus on their interpretation of the text, not just on their artistic talent.
- Good readers need to take time to read the visuals accompanying the text.
- Good readers learn how to read for what information they need.
- Good readers do not have to read visuals in one order.
- Good readers talk about the details in the visual information to help them analyze it.

Things to Talk About to Learn about Visual Literacy

1. the appropriate text to use
2. how to read a graphic layout
3. the meaning that visuals provide
4. whether the reader has to start exactly where he or she left off
5. walking backwards through the text
6. how text may be incomplete without visual support
7. how to read for what we need; skimming and scanning
8. to focus on interpretation and not just artistic talent
9. about the details in the illustration that help you analyze thinking
10. when you need to draw what the story means to you, not just your favorite scene

Say It Fast!

The leader of the Daily Letter has the students say the words in the list fast. The students share some of the strategies they used to read these particular words.

Strategy at a Glance

What: Introduce the Say It Fast strategy.
Why: Introduce this strategy as a way to become a better reader,
How: • Introduce the words in isolation below the text on the Daily Letters.
- Share how good readers examine all the speech sounds and link the letters of each new word so they can pronounce it. Demonstrate with a short list of words taken from the text of the Daily Letter. Say the first word slowly, and think about how you say each part of the word.
- Once the students have looked and said the word slowly from beginning to end cue them, "Say it fast!"
- Talk briefly about how good readers have to put words back together after they have been sounded out.

Think-alouds for Word Study

- Good readers have a systematic way of looking at words, and think about words rather than just acquiring or memorizing a collection of known words.
- Good readers think about how the letters in a word looks from left to right. Eye-spelled words have to look right.
- Good readers think about how letter in a word sounds. Ear-spelled words have to sound right.
- Good readers think about what the little words in bigger words mean.
- Good readers segment words, put the segments back together, and say it fast.

Strategies to Read Words

1. sound out individual letters or letter clusters
2. use base words to analyze parts
3. analyze words left to right
4. try new words
5. notice letter patterns

6. play with words
7. have fun with words
8. say words fast
9. say words slow
10. say words over and over to practise them

30-second Talk

The leader of the Daily Letter has the students practise their response to the prompt with a partner for 30 seconds. The students share their responses.

Strategy at a Glance

What: Introduce the 30-second Talk strategy.

Why: Introduce this strategy as a method to become a better speaker.

How: • Introduce the Ask Me . . . prompt.
  • Assign roles for a Timer/Listener and Speaker.
  • Have the students practise their response to the prompt for 30 seconds in small groups or partners.
  • Have partners or groups of four students take turns practising responding to the prompt for 30 seconds.
  • Have several volunteers perform their 30-second talks with the class
  • Share some of the characteristics of good speakers the students demonstrate.

Think-alouds for 30-second Talk

- Good speakers shift their own body position so everyone can see and hear them in their audience. They speak clearly.
- Good speakers put thought and effort into what they want to say; like writers, they choose their words carefully.
- Good listeners have quiet hands and look at the person speaking.
- Good listeners take the time to seek clarification from the speaker if needed.

TOP TEN

Strategies that Good Speakers Use

1. thinking about what you wanted to say
2. looking at the listeners
3. looking around at the different members of the community
4. speaking clearly
5. remaining steady on your feet
6. having quiet hands (not moving around)
7. smiling
8. relaxing
9. pausing from time to time
10. using a good voice

Strategies for Using the Back of the Daily Letter

Three Stars and a Wish

The leader of the Daily Letter asks the students to make some comments about the different aspects of the Daily Letter itself, or of the sharing of the Daily Letter that day. This strategy is to be used intermittently.

Strategy at a Glance

What: Introduce the Three Stars and a Wish strategy.

Why: Introduce this as a method of self-assessment, or assessment of the leader or members of the story-sharing community.

How: • Have students identify three things they have done well and one thing they wish they could change a bit.
  • Have students share their three stars and a wish with their partner.
  • After students become familiar with the strategy, have them access the leader of the Daily Letter by suggesting the students identify three things the leader has done well and one thing they need to work on.
  • Have the teacher or students use this strategy informally one-to-one during school or at home.

What: • Share this space on the Daily Letter for comments by the teacher or parents about the student, the topics, or the goings-on with the class.

See It, Say It, Check It

The leader of the Daily Letter dictates some words for the students to print or write on the lines of the back of the Daily Letter. The students see, say, write, and check the words as a group, and talk about the interesting aspects of them.

Strategy at a Glance

What: Introduce the See It, Say It, Check It strategy.

Why: Introduce the strategy as a way to write or spell words.

How: • See it: Write a word on the blackboard selected from the Daily Letter text.
  • Say it: Say the word slowly. Have the students say it together slowly.
  • Write it: Have the students look at it and write it down on the line on the back of the Daily Letter.
  • Talk together about the known and unknown parts of the word, the spelling, the meaning, the important parts, and unusual parts of it.
  • Have students check their own words and words of their shoulder partners.
  • Have students visualize the word in their minds.
  • Repeat for each of the words you are sharing.

TOP TEN

Goals of Spelling Word Study

1. forming letters easily and quickly
2. writing the most frequently written words quickly and easily
3. writing the sounds you hear in words
4. writing a large number of known words quickly and easily

5. listening and using word parts to construct words
6. using letter–sound relationships in flexible ways to construct words
7. using knowledge of words to construct new words
8. writing words letter by letter, checking on the letter–sound relationship
9. writing words from left to right
10. using spaces between words

Poet Share

The leader/author of the Daily Letter has the students read the poem and discuss ways to read it, what it is about, and what the leader/author thought about to write the poem. Read the poem several times remind your students it often takes several readings of a poem to absorb the dense imagery in it. Talk about some ways to read the poem.

Strategy at a Glance

What: Introduce the Poet Share strategy.
Why: Introduce this strategy as a way to become a better poet.
How: • Share where you got your ideas for the poem.
    • Share one part of your experience writing the poem.
What: • Add your ideas on what good poets do to the list of what good writers do.
When: • Sometimes, not always, have the students respond to the poem.

Choral Reading

Strategy at a Glance

What: Introduce the Choral Reading strategy.
Why: This strategy allows a student to reinforce information with verbal learning.
How: • Group the students into two groups; one group stands, one group sits
    • Standing group reads line 1 and sits down.
    • Sitting group stands up and reads line 2 and sits down.
    • First group stands, reads line 3, and sits down.
    • Second group stands, reads line 4, and sits down.
    • Groups take turns until poem is finished

TOP TEN

Methods to Talk about a Poem

1. talk about the poem in a small group
2. say the poem four or five different ways by yourself
3. share your reading of the poem with the whole class
4. say the poem as a group
5. say a line per group
6. say a verse per group
7. popcorn read the poem, jumping in and out at any time
8. choral read the poem leaving out predetermined words
9. read the poem silently three or four times
10. chant the poem

Book Pick for more information on Poetry:
Poetry Plus by Meguido Zola

TOP TEN

Ways to Invite Students into Poetry

1. recite poems from heart informally from time to time
2. expose them to the beautiful language of poetry
3. allow time for the multiple readings of the poems
4. encourage students, convince them that they can write poems
5. encourage a personal response to the poem through clustering, sketching, or doodling as they listen and read
6. teach poems that are suitable for the age and interests of the students and others that they may never come across on their own
7. interact personally; join in without dominating
8. create murals around poems to share with the class
9. make emotional connections to the poem; respect their feelings
10. introduce the idea of imagery in the poems

TOP TEN

Questions to Guide a Response to Poetry

1. What is your opinion of the poem?
2. What did you like? dislike?
3. What did you understand? not understand?
4. Does this poem make you think of anything?
5. Do you have any questions about this poem?
6. Can you say what the poem is about in a word, a phrase, or a sentence?
7. How did this poem make you feel?
8. Is there any special part to this poem in the words, ideas, or layout?
9. Is there any connection between this poem and others you have read, or text you have read?
10. What would you say or ask the poet about this poem?

(adapted from Swartz, 1993)

Don'ts for working with poetry:
- don't just focus on technique
- don't just focus on critiquing or dissecting the poem
- don't discuss a poem every day; sometimes just read it!
- don't explain the poet every time

Recall, Retell, Relate

The leader of the Daily Letter asks the students to respond to the prompt on the space at the bottom of the Daily Letter page.

Strategy at a Glance

What: Introduce the students to the Reader Response strategy.

Why: Introduce this strategy as a way to become a more critical reader and writer.

How: • Introduce a prompt for the students to respond to.
- Give students some time to put their ideas down on the bottom of the page.
- Ways to share their responses:
  - with a partner
  - with the class
  - go around the room and read the response of a person in each group

Think-alouds for Recall, Retell, Relate

- Good readers have a systematic way of reflecting on their reading.
- Good readers confirm and adjust their predictions.
- Good readers skim back through the text for understanding.
- Good readers locate specific information.
- Good readers summarize the main points.
- Good readers retell.
- Good readers relate.
- Good readers reflect
- Good readers respond to the reading they do.

TOP TEN

Responses to a Daily Letter

1. retelling
2. relating
3. reflecting
4. responding to the text through drawing
5. making inferences
6. summarizing the information
7. discussing the main idea of the genre
8. sharing opinions on what you felt, learned, or wondered
9. citing parts of the text to support your opinions
10. making personal connections

Think-aloud

The students share what thought processes they have come to understand with the Daily Letter sharing that day. The Wild Card activity gives students a choice of how they wish to further explore the topic with yet another mode of representation.

Strategy at a Glance

What: Introduce the students to the Think-aloud strategy
Why: Introduce this strategy as a way to become a more critical reader and writer.
How: • Ask students to think about what they have learned, what was difficult, easy or hard for them about this Daily Letter.
• Have students share their ideas with a neighbor.
• Have students volunteer to share their ideas with the larger group.

TOP TEN

Wild Card Strategies for the Daily Letter

1. word search
2. demonstration
3. field trip
4. cooking demonstration
5. related art activity
6. problem of the day

7. quote of the day
8. sign language beside words in text
9. Blessed Book, favorite book choice
10. drama through role playing, movement, mime, and puppetry

CHAPTER 7

Independent Writing

Activate the dynamics of the story-writing community by introducing the students to the formation of a workshop community to share responsibility with the teacher for the writing that takes place.

From Reading to Writing

Begin the year by sharing teacher-designed Daily Letters. Compose these Daily Letters to expose students to a variety of genres that arise out of your lives together and what you care about: your interests and concerns at home and school, adventures, expertise, pets, collections, scars, special events, celebrations, trips, guests, discoveries, and wonderings. This is the first step in creating the story-sharing community.

After students have settled into our routine of sharing Daily Letters for several weeks, invite them to compose a number of Daily Letters to celebrate their interests, knowledge, and concerns, to discover their own subjects/topics and control the language and format. Model ways to have them express their learning in a variety of modes such as text, graphics, poetry, and /or demonstrations.

Besides initiating the sharing of writing through Daily Letter language experiences, your other major task is to create the story-writing community. Your goal is to give the students time to participate in a writer's workshop to develop their abilities as writers. Encourage students to find a variety of topics, formats, and partners to write Daily Letters of their choice with. Shortly, perhaps by October, you will be able to introduce them to the idea that they can contribute to, and share responsibility with you for leading, the Daily Letter.

You will be on your way to using the language and writing of students as the major and continuing resource in the classroom for the crafting of Daily Letters. Students begin to live up to the guiding principle of the workshop, that students do think deepest and best when it about something that matters to them.

The Challenges To Become Successful Writers

We create a powerful writer's workshop community by challenging our students to become successful writers of a variety and number of genres on the Daily Letter. We encourage them to tell and write stories from their lives and to polish them into personal touchstones (Calkins, 1986). Share with students the important idea that a successful writer is a person who conveys information, ideas, and experiences clearly to others (Murray, 1968). Share the important idea that the purpose of the Daily Letter is to make them successful writers.

Set the challenge for students to become successful writers in two ways. First, challenge them to discover their subject, to choose an idea, experience, or information that they care about and to transfer it into the minds of the story-sharing community. Secondly, challenge them to design a format that most effectively communicates their ideas, experiences, or information to the minds of the other students.

Students will become successful writers by representing their ideas and understanding in a variety of formats. It may be through a genre such as a poem, a recipe, personal narrative, expository text, or a persuasive reader's response. Impress upon them that it is not the genre that will indicate that they are successful writers, but rather the effectiveness with which they take their idea and transfer it into the minds of the other students. Clarify for them that the student who writes a good collection of jokes and riddles is as much an effective writer as a student composing a personal narrative. The student conducting reflective research is as much an effective writer as the student conducting an informative interview. Cultivate the idea that the choice of genre may increase the clarity of their ideas for the reader.

It will be necessary to support students as they go through the writing process in which they often suffer from the dissonance of not knowing what to write about and how to write it. Celebrate their ability to discover their ideas and to find ways to organize their topics as hallmarks of successful writers.

Creating a Community of Writers

There are a number of important things I do at the beginning of the year to create the story-writing community. The simplest and most effective is to tell lots of personal stories. I encourage my students to tell their stories too. It isn't long before we have a rich collection of special stories. I like to take lots of time to talk at the beginning of the year. There will be plenty of time to write later.

When you take the time to share personal stories, ideas, and interests, as a class you become very close. When your concerns are voiced now through talking together, and later through the students crafting and sharing the Daily Letter, you all become infinitely more connected and caring about one another. The students will bring more of themselves to the class and you, and you will bring more of yourself to them. You make a difference to each other's lives.

TOP TEN

Things to Remember when Teaching Writing

1. provide time for students to write
2. provide a predictable routine
3. provide lots of flexibility of choice of format; encourage risk-taking
4. encourage collaborative writing
5. encourage students to write about what they know about
6. encourage students to keep all their writing
7. remember the writing goes through all the writing stages
8. remember writing is an approximation of adult texts
9. remember your writers need to be heard
10. remember to share the writing strategies your students are using

---

Engage your students to become successful writers with two challenges:

1. Give them choice of what they want to say, to discover their subject on their own.
2. Give them the choice of how they want to say it, to design a format themselves.

Don't provide prompts on writing topics for your students, as it would communicate that you think they do not have the ability to come up with stories on their own.

Book Pick for more information on Teaching Writing:
The Art of Teaching Writing by Lucy McCormick Calkins

Writing Poetry

Engage your students to become successful poets with two challenges:
1. Give them choice of what they want to say, to discover their subject on their own.
2. Give them the choice of how they want to say it, to design a poem format themselves.

We create a powerful writer's workshop community by challenging our students to become successful poets of a variety of poems on the Daily Letter. Like other genres for the Daily Letter, poetry gives them a chance to tell and write from their lives and to polish their writing into personal touchstones. Share with students the important idea that a successful poet is a person who conveys information, ideas, and experiences to others. Share the important idea that the purpose of the Daily Letter is to make them successful poets.

Set the challenge for students to become successful poets in two ways. First, challenge them to discover their subject, to choose an idea, experience, or information that they care about. Secondly, challenge them to design a format for their poem that most effectively communicates their idea, experience, or information to others.

Early in the year, students have the option of either finding or writing a poem to go with their Daily Letter. It is always a more special occasion to write a poem with a friend or a parent than to find one. Sometimes, however, students may share other writers' poems, or use shape and patterned poems to guide them as apprentice poets.

Formula poems are one way for some children to begin with poetry. However, using formula poems can be a dangerous way to teach students poetry, falling back into the ways traditional genrists once taught a form and students filled in the blanks. Your students are much better off if you expose them to a rich variety of forms on the back of the Daily Letter. These poems can be used to mentor students, to give them some ideas for their own poetry writing without providing them with the explicit teaching of a format. You can then give them an open invitation to adapt a poem without formally teaching them a formula.

Beginning poetry formats support the creative process as capable students take the form, run with it, and leave it behind in rather short order. It is a worthy writing goal at this point to continue to encourage students to invent their own poetry. Empower them with the invitation to discover their own poetry subject and format just as you do with other genres of writing. Do not set topics or formats, but encourage them to notice some of the following:

- the kinds of thoughts and imaginings they have
- a look inward to the memories they have
- what they care deeply about to develop an awareness of themselves
- who they care deeply about to develop an awareness of others
- what images they have that represent a state of mind
- what strong feelings they have
- what concerns they have
- what experience is so close to them that they can feel it, they know it well

Immersing students in poetry is the most important learning "layer" for primary students; "response" is the next important layer; and the guiding of them towards the analyzing of the craft will typically come later (Chapman, 1997).

The Daily-Letter Writing Workshop

The Daily Letter centres/writer's workshop is modeled after the highly structured method of literacy instruction of Donald Graves (1983), Lucy Calkins (1986), and

Nancie Atwell (1987). It is designed to replicate the original workshop model and methods set out by these educators in giving students large blocks of time for choice writing. While the model is flexible and designed to allow teachers to personalize it, I believe a close adherence to the original model is useful to create a rich literacy-learning environment that apprentice literacy learners need and deserve. See BLM #18 page 115.

TOP TEN

Conditions of the Writer's Workshop

1. a time for authentic writing experiences
2. holistic language learning
3. experiential
4. open-ended, challenging
5. student-centred
6. large blocks of time
7. social, collaborative
8. active literacy learning
9. democratic
10. shared responsibility of the teacher and students for teaching and learning

When the steps of the writing process (BLM #19 page 116) are combined with the components of the Daily Letter, we find ourselves with a format for crafting Daily Letters in the context of writing workshops or literacy centres.

Steps of the Writing the Daily Letter		Components of the Daily Letter
Front:	Prewriting, Formatting	1. Author, Title, Genre
		3. Graphics
	Drafting, Writing	2. Text
	Reading Word Study	4. Reading Word Study (decoding)
	Ask Me… Prompt	5. Ask Me… Prompt
Back:	Writing Word Study	7. Writing Word Study (encoding)
	Poem	8. Poetry, Song or Chant
	Reader Response	9. Written Response/Reflection
	Publishing	10. Wild Card: choice component

Prewriting

Take a moment to notice or question an image, a memory, a word, a phrase, a sentence, an idea, a treasure, or a story.

TOP TEN

Choices for your Students to Make in their Writing

1. what they want to write about
2. format, genre they want to use for their text
3. format of their Daily Letter
4. Wild Card for their Daily Letter sharing
5. who to work with
6. where to work

Functions of Writing on the Daily Letter

Instrumental/self-maintaining: to satisfy needs and wants, protect self and interests
Examples: biographies, expert talks, interest inventories

Directing: to monitor actions, control actions, get things done
Examples: classroom rules, expectations, opinions, quotations, rules, Daily Letter procedures, clean-up procedures, keeping track of what needs to be done, procedures for science experiments; make plans, give directions; instructions, schedules, metacognitive explanations; requests, persuasive writing, arguments, defending oneself

Personal/expressive: to discover self, express feelings, opinions
Examples: personal experiences, personal responses, stories; biographies, all-about-me stories and poems; learning logs; opinions on events or experiences

Interactive/interpersonal: to maintain social relationships
Examples: invitations, friendships, thank-yous, ceremonies, rituals, birthdays, celebrations, special events; field trips, greetings, concert programs

Imaginative/creative: to engage in pretend or make-believe
Examples: stories, dramas, role plays, writing in role (imagine you are…); scripts, reader's theatre; art demonstrations, posters; invitations to write, ABC books, fables, legends, yarns

Representational/informative: to communicate information
Examples: instructions, labeling, telling, retelling, factual reports, explaining processes; story maps or story webs; science or social studies reports

Divertive/entertaining: to enjoy, amuse oneself and others
Examples: word play, jokes, riddles, puns, amusing events, situations; nursery rhymes, jingles, chants, songs, raps, poetry

Perpetuating/recording: to record events, ideas, and feelings
Examples: store of ideas, reminders; real-world issues, special events, traveling journals; record notes

Heuristic/epistemic: to acquire knowledge and understanding
Examples: inquiries; ask questions, record data, problems, solutions; articles, essays, stories; before/during/after stories, predictions, wonders, hypotheses; science experiments, demonstrations; close procedures of various genres, reviews; recalling/remembering, reflecting on learning processes, metacognitive explanations; reasoning, expanding, clarifying, analyzing, interpreting, evaluating ideas and information, comparing/contrasting, drawing conclusions

Steps of the Writing Process

Prewriting

- Discover a subject: Have writers search for their writing idea, experience, or information to share. Have them discover and write about what they know and care about.
- Sense the audience: Have writers plan to write their own ideas with their intended audience in mind, to be conscious of their audiences. Have them realize that they have to consider whether the reader will be able to understand what they are saying. They need to learn to recognize their audience.
- Search for specifics: Have writers search for the material for subject and intended audience within themselves and from others, books, the Internet. Have them find the details of the subject they are focused on.

Formatting

- Create a design for your Daily Letter: Have writers create the design for their Daily Letter.

Writing

- Draft
- Write: Have writers collect their ideas, experiences, information in a notebook or writing folder.

After Writing

- Edit and Proofread
- Develop a creative, critical eye: Have writers develop their writing; cultivate their use of the "precious particles" of good writing through their writing conferences with you. Work with students to make their writing clear and stylish.
- Rewrite: Have writers rewrite parts of their genre to make it work. Conference your students again and make the final approval for publishing.

Publishing

- Assemble each of the components of the Daily Letter and publish the final design of the Daily Letter: Have writers prepare the final design to share with the story-sharing community. Work with your students on the choices they make.
- Share the Daily Letter: Do not judge your students' writing choices. Work with them.
- Keep a portfolio of the Daily Letters you have made.

(adapted from Murray, 1968).

Book Pick for more information on Building a Storying Community: *Story Works* by David Booth and Bob Barton (2000)

7. think-aloud strategies to share
8. demonstrations to support their Daily Letter sharing
9. which day to share
10. roles and responsibilities of others during their Daily Letter sharing

Formatting

Think about a format that communicates your thinking, your experience. Decide on the format for your idea.

TOP TEN

Shapes and Sizes for Stories on the Daily Letter

1. stories from within, at home, or on the playground
2. tales and legends
3. personal stories, novels
4. reader's theatre scripts
5. advertisements
6. daydreams
7. gossip
8. anecdotes
9. troubles, mournings
10. celebrations

Graphics

Decide if your text will benefit from some graphics that will further develop your idea or add meaning to it.

TOP TEN

Ways to Integrate Graphics with Text

1. photographs, clip art, pictures
2. charts, graphs, maps
3. webs, time lines
4. window panes
5. indexes
6. tables, data charts, diagrams, maps
7. friezes, banners
8. posters
9. plot organizers
10. spread sheets, graphs

Book Pick for more information on Visual Literacy: *I See What You Mean* by Steve Moline

Writing/Drafting

Create your text. Take your draft to a writing conference. Print, write, or word-process parts of your Daily Letter.

Reading Word Study

List six to eight words from your text on the front of the Daily Letter. Decide on why these words are important: Do they have a pattern? Are they tricky to read?

Book Pick for more information on Word Lists:
The Reading Teacher's Book of Lists, Fourth Edition by Fry et al

TOP TEN

Types of Words for Decoding Word Study

1. high-frequency words
2. Dolch Words
3. difficult words from previous reading
4. problem words
5. sight words
6. subject words
7. new words
8. phonograms (*-ab, -ace, -ack, –act, -ade,* etc.)
9. word families
10. fun words

Ask Me… Prompt

Create an Ask Me… prompt for your Daily Letter, to get the readers to display what they learned from it.

TOP TEN

Ask Me…? Prompts for the Daily Letter

1. Ask me to draw you a picture about…
2. Ask me what I think about…
3. Ask me to give a reason for…
4. Ask me to relate my favorite part of the…
5. Ask me to retell… , or tell about…
6. Ask me to reflect on…
7. Ask me to clarify…
8. Ask me to describe…
9. Ask me to explain…
10. Ask me to imagine…

Writing Word Study

Choose six to eight words from the text on the front of the Daily Letter. You will dictate to the class to write on the lines on the back of the Daily Letter. Decide why these words are important.

TOP TEN

Types of Words for Students to Listen To, List, Look At

1. useful words
2. spelling demons
3. patterned words

4. phonograms
5. related words
6. irregular words
7. homophones
8. confusing words
9. root words, words with suffixes
10. key vocabulary

Poetry

Write or find a poem that goes with your Daily Letter. Decide why this poem, song, or chant matters to you.

TOP TEN

Things to Think about when Writing a Poem

1. look of the poem
2. shape/length of the poem
3. sound of the poem
4. pattern of the poem
5. beat of the poem
6. rhyme of the poem
7. topic of the poem
8. feeling of the poem
9. images of the poem
10. seriousness/novelty of the poem

Book Picks for more information on Poetry:
Leap Into Poetry by Avis Harley
Classroom Events Through Poetry by Larry Schwartz

Reader Response

Decide a response you want the readers to make to the text.

TOP TEN

Prompts for Retelling, Relating, and Reflecting

1. I especially like…
2. I noticed…
3. I feel that…
4. This is about…
5. I remember…
6. This reminds me of….
7. This makes me think of…; It's hard to believe…
8. Now I want to know…; I wonder if…
9. Now I understand…
10. What do you think about…?

Publishing

After your final writing conference with the teacher, organize each of your components of the Daily Letter onto the Daily Letter template, cut and paste them using the computer or by hand.

Make a class set of your Daily Letter. Hole punch the copies and make a transparency of your text. Confirm your day to share your Daily Letter.

TOP TEN

Preparations to Share the Daily Letter

1. have each component of the Daily Letter finished and checked
2. have the Daily Letter published copy finalized by the teacher
3. consider the audience in preparing to share the text
4. take ample rehearsal time alone, in a small group, at home
5. decide when you are ready to do her Daily Letter
6. be given teacher support and feedback during practice (conference)
7. sign up to share Daily Letter
8. prepare materials, such as overhead transparency
9. review the steps in sharing the Daily Letter
10. organize prompts for use with the Daily Letter sharing

TOP TEN

Things NOT to Publish on the Daily Letter

1. embarrassing stories about others
2. unauthorized stories
3. stories with offensive language
4. violent crime stories
5. long stories (publish these as books)
6. illegible stories
7. plagiarized stories
8. unedited stories
9. unfinished stories
10. stories written in haste

CHAPTER 8

Assessment and Evaluation

We can assess our students' literacy learning by systematically observing what they do with their Daily Letters, what they say about their Daily Letters, and what they make of their Daily Letters. Thus, there are three parts to the assessment and evaluation of our students' understanding of literacy through the Daily Letter:

> What they do—their process learning of the Daily Letter
> What they say—their conversations and writing of their understanding
> What they make—the Daily Letters as artifacts of their learning

Creating a self-directed, independent community of learners is at times difficult to manage, but well worth the effort, considering the rich assessment data we collect on our students at this time. It is through this quality time with our students that we begin to form a personal mentor relationship with them. It is through this relationship that we begin to nurture their reflective practice about their literacy learning.

TOP TEN

Strategies to Assess and Evaluate the Daily Letter

1. collect student performance data daily through observation of the Daily Letter
2. set routines to both formally and informally collect student performance data
3. take action with students as their needs arise
4. make summaries of their performance of their Daily Letter on Snapshot Observation Grid and checklist
5. share your understanding of various aspects of students' progress in informal conversations
6. share your understanding of the students' progress with parents at a three-way conference
7. align the assessment of the Daily Letter with the written curriculum and actual instruction
8. check students' understanding by conducting individual reading and writing assessment conferences each week
9. have your students routinely monitor their own learning progress through the use of performance standards
10. use portfolios to organize the writing and published Daily Letter of your students

Observing the Learning Process

Since the Daily Letter covers each of the components of a comprehensive literacy-learning plan, you have a valuable opportunity to notice a whole range of knowledge, skills, concept development, and attitudes of students during the routine hour-long (half-hour for early primary classes) session of the Daily Letter.

Observe students as they are reading the text aloud, silently, or in unison. Observe how they talk about the text and the visual graphics to support the text. Observe how they decode and encode words, and make analogies between that day's text and previously viewed texts. View how they are sharing poetry, and reflecting in oral and written form on the story. All of these kid-watching activities provide a steady source of valuable informal assessment data on literacy learners and on what aspect of the Daily Letter you need to put more energy into. View your students to both assess their progress and achievement, and to inform your teaching practice.

When students become the leaders of their own Daily Letters you are in an even better position to collect and interpret information about your students' literacy-learning abilities, and to inform your teaching. This role of sharing responsibility with the students for the teaching and learning of the Daily Letter affords you a unique vantage point to more effectively observe what each child is doing (process of sharing the Daily Letter), saying (discussions about the Daily Letter), and making (Daily Letter Artifact) of their Daily Letters. When you are freed from the lead teaching role, you can focus on being the assessor, and thus are in a better position to do this with sensitivity and accuracy. You will have the unique position of being able to make many considerations about students. You can assess

- levels of confidence
- energy
- attitudes towards reading/writing
- attitudes towards themselves as writers/readers
- attitudes towards poetry
- attitudes towards themselves as poets
- reading/writing preferences, topics and formats
- metacognition and metalinguistic awareness
- effectiveness of communication
- inquiry and exploration of topics of interest
- writing processes
- writing strategies
- writing skills
- reading processes
- reading strategies
- reading skills
- repertoire of genres and forms of representation
- reading/writing across the curriculum
- progress and performance (achievement)
- meaning-making through reading and writing

Assessing the Process of Learning Literacy

With the Daily Letter we have routine opportunities to observe the processes students go through to craft and share their Daily Letters. You will have numerous occasions to observe what they do individually with the Daily Letter and with the larger group.

You can assess what students do as readers
- reading a read-aloud
- reading the Daily Letter
- reading material of choice
- reading words in isolation on the Word Study
- reading poetry on the Daily Letter
- reading poetry of choice

You can assess what students do as writers
- writing the Daily Letter
- writing in their journals or notebooks
- writing the words of the Writing Word Study
- writing a response to an aspect of the Daily Letter
- writing a comment
- writing a compliment

You can assess what students do as speakers
- speaking during a read-aloud
- speaking as a leader during a Daily Letter
- speaking as a member of the class during the Daily Letter
- speaking in a small group
- speaking one-on-one

You can assess what students do as listeners
- listening to other students talk
- listening to the teacher
- listening to the sounds of words in the Writing Word Study

Recording Observations

Ideally the text of the Daily Letter should be difficult enough for a student to make some mistakes. You want them to make mistakes because you want to see what they do as they are making them. You want to see if they are self-correcting, or making mistakes without noticing it. If you know what these mistakes are, you can plan your instruction to improve their oral reading.

We use different kinds of observation recording sheets when we are assessing students as they work to process their understanding of the Daily Letter. We use a number of assessment instruments. Some focus on a general glance at a number of students in a short period of time. Other forms of assessment zero in much more closely on the behavior of one student. They are all valuable assessment tools. We want to use a variety of them over the course of a reporting period.

Snapshot Observation Recording Sheets

The Snapshot Observation sheet (BLM #20 page 124) is a simple, one-page grid made up of enough boxes for each of our students (adapted from Chapman, 1997). I put the names of the students in the boxes in alphabetical order by first name and make photocopies of it. This makes it easier for me to get new information down quickly without losing time looking for the right name to put the information it! There is a line at the top of the page for important information such as the date and time. I also make a note of the context of the observation so several weeks from now the information with make sense to me. Before each

Snapshot Observation Grid

Date: _____ Time: _____ Context:_____

Name: _____	Name: _____	Name: _____	Name: _____	Name: _____
Name: _____	Name: _____	Name: _____	Name: _____	Name: _____
Name: _____	Name: _____	Name: _____	Name: _____	Name: _____
Name: _____	Name: _____	Name: _____	Name: _____	Name: _____
Name: _____	Name: _____	Name: _____	Name: _____	Name: _____
Name: _____	Name: _____	Name: _____	Name: _____	Name: _____

reporting period I will take some time to transfer the information gathered here to a file that I have for each individual child.

Checklists

A checklist (BLMs #21 page 126 and #22 page 127) is the second kind of observation sheet. It can record one student's progress or the entire class. Many school districts provide lists of the objectives, goals, or learning outcomes of the students at each grade level. We use checklists as an efficient method to record assess a child's general progress in their reading or writing, or their specific process in writing a particular genre for the Daily Letter.

In-depth Observation Sheet

The last kind of observation sheet is a focused in-depth observation sheet (BLMs #23 page 128 and #24 page 129) on the leader of the Daily Letter event. I select the student who will be leading the Daily Letter as the person I will shadow, to make a detailed assessment of his or her leading of the shared literacy event. I use a formal recording sheet to make a comprehensive examination of their presentation. I will share this information with them in a conference during the afternoon literacy centres.

Conversations and Conferences

Conversations

We can assess the progress and achievement of our literacy learners through conversation with them. Take time with individual or small groups of students to have meaningful conversations with them about how they are doing. Listen attentively to them and ask questions about their understandings.

With the Daily Letter, you have routine opportunities to enter into conversations about the crafting and sharing of their Daily Letters. You have ample occasions to converse with students about their literacy learning, and many sources of this information:

- formal conversations with whole class during the Daily Letter
- informal conversations with the whole class during read-alouds and centre/workshop time
- formal conversations in small groups
- informal conversations in small groups
- reading and writing conference or one-on-one

Conferences

The prime value of the afternoon literacy centres or writer's workshop is that they afford us time to converse with individual learners to find out how they are doing. Listening to students is an important means of assessing their language abilities. Examining what they write is another informative way to learn about their understandings. When you sit and talk with a student at a conference, you can clarify questions about their thinking. Spend time conversing with them to help determine their attitude towards literacy learning and the progress they are making.

I will show a student what I am writing about them if they ask me. It is important for them to know what they need to attend to if they have areas they need to grow in. How can we expect our students to move in new directions in their learning if we do not communicate with them the direction they need to go!

Assessment Checklist of Writing for Daily Letter

Name: _____   Date: _____

Criteria	Emergent	Developing	Exceeding	Comments
Selects topic				
Easy start to writing				
Writing flows				
Ideas developed				
Makes sense				
Variety of sentences				
Choice of words				
Punctuation				
Spelling				
Understands phonics				
Editing				
Proofreading				
Rewriting				

Checklist of Daily Letter Strategies

Name: _____   Date: _____

Strategy	Difficulty using strategy	Ability to use strategy	Independent use of strategy	Comments
Author Share				
Genre Share				
Activating Prior Knowledge				
Silent Support				
Coding the Text				
Word Wall				
Visualization				
Say It Fast!				
30-second Talk				
See It, Say It, Check It				
Poetry Share				
Reader Response				
Think-aloud				

In-depth Observation Sheet: Crafting the Daily Letter

Name: _____ Date: _____

Component	Two Stars	Wish	Comments
Intro. Author			
Genre			
Text Read			
Coding			
Visuals			
Word Study			
Ask Me...			
Poetry			
Word Study			
Wild Card			
Other			

In-depth Observation Sheet: Sharing the Daily Letter

Name: _____   Date: _____

Component	Two Stars	Wish	Comments
Intro. Author			
Genre			
Text Read			
Coding			
Visuals			
Word Study			
Ask Me...			
Poetry			
Word Study			
Wild Card			
Other			

Scheduling regular individual conferences provides valuable learning opportunities for both you and the students. You learn about them, and they learn about themselves and the assessment and evaluation process. You deepen and enrich understandings together.

I try to have conferences with five of my literacy learners each day. By the end of the week I have had conversations with each one of the students in the class.

Goal Setting

While we take the lead role in assessing the individual learners, we need to also involve the students in the process as well. Share the responsibility for the assessment and evaluation with students in the same way that you share responsibility for the teaching and learning of the Daily Letter. You want your students to be thoughtful individuals who reflect upon and evaluate their own literacy learning.

Make sure that the pathway to success is not a mystery to them. Put your students in control of their development as you participate with them in conferences to share evidence of growth in their literacy practices. It is your responsibility to help them see specifically what they have accomplished and what they need to work on. You want them to keep records of their progress and the goals you have set together each week.

An effective way to involve students in self-evaluation is to teach them how to assess their own reading and writing using a set criteria or standard to measure their work against. We use rubrics and our observations of the Daily Letters to help them understand the hallmarks of quality reading and writing. A rubric is an effective tool for students to measure or grade their writing for the Daily Letter (BLM #25 page 131). To assess performance in literacy, use rubrics, or rating scales, with four levels of proficiency numbered from 1 to 4: 1 is the lowest standard and 4 is the highest standard.

If students can begin to use the language (criteria) around the performance standards you have set together, they can become agents of their development as successful readers and writers. Performance standard descriptors are a powerful method to provide the language for students, teachers, and parents to talk about the students' writing and set specific goals to improve it.

Students should have their own copies of the rubrics they are working with. These rubrics can be stored with the Daily Letters in the student's portfolio. You can refer to these during writer's workshop or during conferences. You can highlight or put a check mark beside the criteria they meet as you analyze their writing or spelling.

Writers can use these rating scales to set goals for future writing projects. The criteria they do not meet give them valuable information of where they need to go from here. They have a clear, written outline of where they need to go in their literacy practice. These rubrics serve to also inform the teacher and parents of the growth over time of the student as a literate person.

Three-Way Conferences

Considering the collaborative nature of the Daily Letter and the strong home–school connection, it is important that the parents of the students using the Daily Letter also participate in the process to assess and evaluate the growth of their child's literacy understanding. Three-way conferences between the teacher, parent, and child serve as a forum for care givers of the student to gain greater

You will have to decide just when your students are ready to use criteria for self-assessment of their writing against a published standard. When you do start, you need to ensure that the language of the rubric is suitable for the students you are working with. Building the rubric together with students gives it greater meaning to the students.

Rubric For Writing Stories for the Daily Letter

Name: _____

Aspect	1 Underdeveloped	2 Competent	3 Strong	4 Exemplary
Meaning Ideas Form Detail	Doesn't capture reader	Gains readers attention	Sustains readers attention	Hooks reader, high interest throughout
Style Clarity Variety of language Impact of language	Limited language Few details	Uses language appropriately Some details	Uses interesting language Supporting details used	Uses language to create effect Rich use of language Effective use of detail
Form Sequence Characters Setting Dialogue	No clear beginning, middle, and end Limited storyline Sequence difficult to follow Dialogue is confusing	Logical beginning, middle, and end Basic elements of story present Logical order to story Dialogue is clear but characters may sound the same	Logical beginning and middle, and strong end Describes setting and characters Story logical and clear order Dialogue is clear, may sound like it is read	Strong storyline Engaging beginning, middle, and end Well developed setting and mood Strong story line Dialogue is clear, may reveal character
Voice of writer	None	None	Some sense of voice of writer	Strong voice of writer
Conventions	Hard to read Repeated errors	Some errors Parts hard to follow	Few errors Errors do not interfere with meaning	Correct, except for some errors in complex structures, may have special features

insight to how the student is progressing with their literacy learning. Share with the parents the rubrics the students are using, and show them the students' growth over time and present achievement. Students can share their understanding of their rubrics with their parents at these conferences.

Complimenting Learners

We create a powerful story-sharing community by immersing our students in regular communication and feedback on their efforts and achievement. We can accomplish this by writing a line or two of comment, or a Three Stars and a Wish compliment, on the back of the Daily Letter. We can also invite the parents of our students to also use the Three Stars and a Wish strategy to write comments or compliments with or for their child or teacher.

I use the Daily Letter to teach students to write informative comments and compliments, and to foster self-efficacy without the use of rewards and reading incentive programs. This community of story-sharing must be self-organizing to enhance learning. The participation of our students should be self-sustaining. For these reasons I find it is not advisable to use a reward system. I support my students' participation through discussion around how they are doing, not by sticking stickers on their Daily Letter page. I want to show interest in my students as an editor to facilitate their improvement by having authentic conversations about what they can work on.

Students can learn to become more intentional readers and writers through spending time talking about 3S–3P; i.e., praise that is sincere, specific, and sufficient, and properly given for praiseworthy success in the preferred manner by the learner (Wlodkowski, 1985). Make your praise

Sincere
Specific
Sufficient
Properly given
Praiseworthy
in **P**referred manner

TOP TEN

Ways to Give Students Feedback and Reinforcement with the Daily Letter

1. give your students immediate feedback if you can
2. acknowledge correct responses
3. relate feedback to the group learning goals
4. give praise and other verbal /nonverbal reinforcement for thinking
5. make use of peer evaluation techniques
6. assign nightly practice of the Daily Letter
7. see that parents are involved with students' progress
8. train students to provide sincere and specific feedback to their peers
9. use praise sparingly and never when unmerited
10. corroborate accurate responses of students

I believe our time is too valuable to spend it giving out stickers that lead to some short-term goals that value extrinsic motivation and focus on competitive performances. I believe our role is to teach our students to have their own goals, to get a little bit better each day with the self directing of their own learning, not because they think someone will give them a prize.

Assessing the Daily Letter

Each student will make 10 to 20 Daily Letters over the course of the school year. These Daily Letters are artifacts representing their understanding of literacy. With these products, you have 10 to 20 opportunities to assess and evaluate their present understanding of literacy.

Observation of the Daily Letter as an product of literacy learning reveals a great deal about the concepts, skills, and strategies students use, and their knowledge of conventions of print, spelling, and punctuation. It also tells much about their ability to organize their ideas on paper and in front of a group. The Daily Letter product may be used to assess the student's abilities to read, write, and respond.

Use individual recording sheets (BLMs #23 page 128 and #24 page 129) to make notes about the students' presentation of each component of the Daily Letter. Write anecdotal comments or use a checklist and coding system that identifies if the student is able to work independently on it, needs some support, or requires further attention. Use a holistic scoring rubric that gives a rating of the Daily Letter as a whole, or ones that examine the individual components such as text, graphics, word studies, or written responses.

Daily Letter Portfolios

Each student includes all Daily Letters to date in a folder. This is not just a work folder, but a purposeful collection of what the student knows and can do. It is a process folio because it documents the students' writing and learning process. This collection serves as a record of a student's growth over time.

Each Daily Letter in the collection is accompanied by an entry slip (BLM #26 page 135) to document any important information the student wants to note about the particular artifact, and a rubric to document the rating of it.

Additional items in the portfolio can provide students with the opportunity for self-assessment (BLM #27 page 136), the opportunity to reflect on their relationship with the Daily Letter event (BLM #28 page 137), and a means of record-keeping (BLM #29 page 138).

Informal Assessment

We create a powerful story-sharing community by creating a routine of finding moments to informally assess students as we pass by their desks during the day. Ask a student to quickly read the list of sight words on the bottom of the Daily Letter. Have another child recite the poem or share the strategies they use to read a word they are having trouble with. In the morning, quickly scan everyone's Daily Letter to see if parents have signed or made comments on the previous day's Daily Letter. Parents who cannot, or do not, take responsibility for the sharing of the Daily Letter at home can be replaced with a cross-grade tutor who comes in each day to review the Daily Letter with students, sign it, and leave it on their desks.

TOP TEN

Questions for Assessing the Sharing of the Daily Letter

1. Did the students understand the Daily Letter?
2. To what extent did the students understand the Daily Letter?
3. Who read it fluently?
4. Did students self-correct when reading?
5. What parts were easy? What parts were hard? For whom?
6. Was there evidence of problem-solving being used?
7. Did the level of the text accomplish what you wanted it to? How do you know this?
8. What do you need to drop out of emphasis on the next Daily Letter?
9. What do you need to keep working on?
10. What do the students need more experiences with?

Entry Slips for Daily Letter Portfolio

Entry Slip

Name: _____

Date: _____

Daily Letter:_____

What I would like you to notice:

Entry Slip

Name: _____

Date: _____

Daily Letter:_____

What I would like you to notice:

Entry Slip

Name: _____

Date: _____

Daily Letter:_____

What I would like you to notice:

Entry Slip

Name: _____

Date: _____

Daily Letter:_____

What I would like you to notice:

Entry Slip

Name: _____

Date: _____

Daily Letter:_____

What I would like you to notice:

Entry Slip

Name: _____

Date: _____

Daily Letter:_____

What I would like you to notice:

Portfolio Self-Assessment

My very best Daily Letter is _____

I feel this is my best because

My best writing is _____

Other Daily Letters that are special to me:

These are my best Daily Letters because

Daily Letter Reflections

My thoughts on myself as a writer:

My thoughts on myself as a reader:

My thoughts on myself as a leader:

My thoughts on myself as a member of the Daily Letter community:

Daily Letter Record Keeping

Daily Letter #___: _____

Comments, Compliments, Concerns:

Daily Letter #___: _____

Comments, Compliments, Concerns:

Daily Letter #___: _____

Comments, Compliments, Concerns:

Daily Letter #___: _____

Comments, Compliments, Concerns:

Daily Letter #___: _____

Comments, Compliments, Concerns:

Daily Letter #___: _____

Comments, Compliments, Concerns:

Conclusion

I am grateful that our Daily Letter community has become a deeply caring, kind community. There has been no hierarchy. Everyone has had equal membership. No one has been in the high or low remedial group, or been sent out of our community to get special help.

I believe that we have met our goals and expectations to share the responsibility for the teaching and learning—together—as a committed story-sharing community. I believe that we have deepened and enriched our own literacy learning through the willingness of all the members to become a resource for each other. Our gathering together to cooperate, collaborate, and celebrate has helped us reach our common goals. We have taken the time, as community members, to meet together with our Daily Letters to share our concerns and successes, to connect to each other, and to recognize that we are all part of a group who value and strengthen each member's contribution.

The Daily Letter has successfully provided a framework for us to participate together as a story-sharing community each day. With the Daily Letter, our school life has mattered, and we have grown independently because we have not been alone.

Classroom teachers are the most important factor in the success or failure of at-risk children in our schools. They are responsible for the minute-by-minute instruction; decisions teachers make, and the kind of instruction and support they provide, make the difference between success and failure. Even in schools with strong instructional support programs and specialist teachers, children spend most of their time with their classroom teachers. For children, classroom teachers maybe the last and best hope for school and life success (Allington & Cunningham, 1999).

Enjoy your time with a unique story-sharing community. Know that when you build such positive classroom dynamics, the literacy learning will be deepened and enriched. It will matter deeply to you, your students, and their parents, and it will satisfy the needs of everyone.

Acknowledgments

The author's profound thanks to
- my mother and father, for having always encouraged me to story
- my husband John, for having always been my hero
- my daughter Alena, for inspiring me to write as she does
- my son Jamie, for his loyal support
- my son Zak, for always caring so much
- my friend and advisor Meguido Zola, for his talented mentorship
- Carolyn Mamchure for her modeling of the art of professional writing
- my advisor Marilyn Chapman, for her dedication to early literacy
- Norma Jansen, for her wisdom about children and faith
- Dinah Phillips, for her wisdom and dedication to literacy
- Selina Millar, for embracing the Daily Letter with older students
- Birgit Neilsen, for inspiring high school students and me, and
- Carole Murphy, whose spirit lives in all of us who dare to care so much

Bibliography

Allington, R., & Cunningham, P. (1999). *Classrooms that work*. New York: Addison-Wesley Longman.

Anderson, R.C., Hiebert, E.H., Scott, J.A. & Wilkinson, I.A.G. (1985). *Becoming a nation of readers: the report of the commission on reading*. Washington, DC: National Institute of Education.

Atwell, N. (1987). *In the middle: writing, reading and learning with adolescents*. Portsmouth, NH: Boynton Cook Publishers.

Au, K.H. (1993). *Literacy in multicultural settings*. Fort Worth, TX: Harcourt, Brace, Jovanovich.

Avery, C. (1993). *...And with a light touch*. Portsmouth, NH: Heinemann.

Bakhtin, M.M. (1979/1986). *Speech and other late essays*. (V. W. McGee, Trans., C. Emmerson & M. Holquist, Eds.). Austin, TX: University of Texas Press.

Booth, D. (Ed.) (1996). *Literacy techniques*. Markham, ON: Pembroke Publishers.

Booth, D. (Ed.) (1996). *Guiding the reading process*. Markham, ON: Pembroke Publishers.

Booth, D., & Barton, B. (2000). *Story works*. Markham, ON: Pembroke Publishers.

Booth, D. (2001). *Reading and writing in the middle years*. Markham, ON: Pembroke Publishers.

British Columbia Ministry of Education (1990). *Primary Program: Foundations Document*. Victoria, BC: British Columbia Ministry of Education.

British Columbia Ministry of Education (2000). *Performance Standards Document*. Victoria, BC: British Columbia Ministry of Education.

Bruner, J. (1990). *Acts of meaning*. Cambridge, MA: Harvard University Press.

Bruner, J. (1996). *The culture of education*. Cambridge, MA: Harvard University Press.

Buis, K. (2002). *The daily letter: redefining, reconceptualizing and reconditioning genre in the elementary classroom*. Vancouver, BC: Simon Fraser University.

Calkins, L. M. (1986). *The art of teaching writing*. Portsmouth, NH: Heinemann.

Calkins, L.M. (1991). *Living between the lines*. Portsmouth, NH: Heinemann.

Calkins, L.M. (1994). *The art of teaching writing (New edition)*. Portsmouth, NH: Heinemann.

Cambourne, B., Fitzsimmon, P., & Geekie, P. (1999). *Understanding literacy development*. Stoke on Trent, UK: Trentham Books.

Chambers, A. (1991). *The reading environment.* Portland, ME: Stenhouse/ Markham, ON: Pembroke Publishers.

Chapman, M.L. (1997). *Webs of meaning: writing in the elementary school.* Toronto, ON: ITP Nelson.

Chapman, M.L. (1999). "Situated, social Active Learning Rewriting genre in the elementary classroom." *Communications,* Vol. 16 No. 4, 469–490.

Clay, M. (1985). *The early detection of early reading difficulties (3rd Edition).* Portsmouth, NH: Heinemann.

Clay, M. (1991). *Becoming literate: The construction of inner control.* Portsmouth, NH: Heinemann.

Clay, M. (1993). *An observation survey of early literacy achievement.* Portsmouth, NH: Heinemann.

Ehri, L.C., & Robbins, C. (1992). "Beginners need some decoding skills to read words by analogy." *Reading Research Quarterly,* 27, 13–26.

Flippo, R.F. (2001). *Reading researchers in search of common ground.* International Reading Association.

Forrester, A., & Reinhard, M. (1990). *The learner's way.* Winnipeg, MB: Peguis

Fountas, I.C., & Pinnell, G.S. (1996). *Guided reading: good first teaching for all children.* Portsmouth, NH: Heinemann.

Freebody, P. (1993). "Socio-cultural approach: resourcing four roles as a literacy learner." In A. Badenhop & A. Watson (Eds.), *Prevention of Reading Failure* (pp. 48–60).

Fry, Donald. (1985). *Children talk about books: Seeing themselves as readers.* Milton Keynes: Open University Press.

Fry, Kress, & Fountoukidis (2000). *The reading teacher's book of lists.* NJ: Prentice Hall.

Fulford, Robert. (1990). *The triumph of narrative.* Toronto, ON: Anansi.

Fu, D., & Townsend, J. (1999). "Serious learning: Language Lost." *Language Arts,* 76(5) 404–411.

Gardner, H. (1983). *Multiple Intelligences: The Theory in Practice.* New York: Basic Books.

Gibbs, J. (1987). *Tribes: a process for social development and cooperative learning.* Santa Rosa, CA: Center Source Publications.

Goodman, K.S. (1978). "Kidwatching: An alternative to testing." *National Elementary School Principal,* 57, 41–45.

Goodman, K. S. (1985). "Kidwatching: observing children in the classroom." In A. Jaggar, and M.T. Smith-Burke (Eds.), *Observing the language learner* Newark, DE: IRA and Urbana, IL: National Council of Teachers of English, 9–18.

Goodman,Y.M., & Wilde, S. (1996). *Notes from a kidwatcher: selected writings of Yetta M. Goodman.* Portsmouth, NH: Heinemann.

Graves, D. (1983). *Writing: teachers and children at work.* Portsmouth, NH: Heinemann.

Graves, D. (1992). *Portfolio portraits.* Portsmouth, NH: Heinemann.

Guthrie, J., & Wigfield, A. (1997). *Reading engagement: motivationg through integrated instruction.* Newark, DE: International Reading Association.

Halliday, Michael. (1975). *Learning how to mean.* New York: Elsevier.

Halliday, M. (1985). *Spoken and written language.* Beelong, Victoria: Deakin University (Republished by Oxford University Press).

Harley, Avis. (2001). *Leap into poetry.* Honesdale, PA: Wordsong/Boyds Mills Press.

Harvey, S., & Goudvis, A. (2000). *Strategies that work: teaching comprehension to enhance understanding.* Portland, ME: Stenhouse.

Heard, G. (1989). *For the good of the earth and sun: teaching poetry.* Portsmouth, NH: Heinemann.

Heard, G. (1999). *Writing toward home.* Portsmouth, NH: Heinemann.

Holdaway, D. (1979). *The foundations of literacy.* Auckland, NZ: Ashton Scholastic.

Holdaway, D. (1974). *Independence in reading.* Auckland, NZ: Ashton Scholastic.

Lambert, (2003). *Leadership capacity for lasting school improvement.* ASCD

Lave, J., & Wenger, E. (1991). *Situated learning legitimate peripheral participation.* Cambridge, UK: Cambridge University Press.

Lewis, C., Schaps, E., (1996). "The caring classroom's academic edge." *Educational Leadership,* 54 (1), 16–21.

Mamchure, Caroline (1997). *Designs for learning: writing. Education 485 Study guide.* Faculty of education and center for distance education. Vancouver, BC: Simon Fraser University.

Mamchure, C. (1990) "But…the curriculum." *Phi delta kappan,* 71(8), 634–637.

McCracken, J., & McCracken, R.A. (1996). *Beyond phonics.* Winnipeg, MN: Peguis.

McGee, L., & Richgels, D. (1996). *Literacy's beginnings (2nd Edition).* Boston, MA: Allyn & Bacon.

Moffat, J. (1992). *Detecting growth in language.* Portsmouth, NH: Heinemann.

Moline, S. (1995). *I see what you mean.* Portland, ME: Stenhouse/Markham, ON: Pembroke Publishers.

Moustafa, M. (1997). *Beyond traditional phonics.* Portsmouth, NH: Heinemann.

Murray, Donald. (1968). *A writer teaches writing: a practical method of teaching composition.* Boston, MA: Houghton Mifflin.

O'Flahavan, J.F., & Seidl, B.L. (1997). "Fostering literate communities in school: a case for socio-cultural approaches to reading instruction." In Stahl & D.A. Hayes (Eds.), *Instructional models for reading.* Mahwah, NJ: Erlbaum, 203–220.

Popp, M.S. (1996). *Teaching language and literature in elementary classrooms.* NJ: Lawrence Erlbaum Associates.

Rogoff, B. (1990). *Apprenticeship in thinking: cognitive development in social contexts.* New York: Oxford University Press.

Rogoff, B., Matusov, E. E., & White, C. (1996). "Models for teaching and learning: participation in a community of learners." In Olson, D. and Torrance, N., *The handbook of Education and Human Development: new models of learning, teaching and schooling.* Cambridge, MA.: Blackwell.

Rosen, Michael. (1989). *The hypnotiser.* London, UK: Andre Deutsch.

Routman, R. (1991). *Invitations: changing as teachers and learners K–12.* Portsmouth, NH: Heinemann.

Santa, C. (1990) "Teaching as research" in *Opening the door to classroom research,* Mary Olsen, Ed. Newark, DE: International Reading Association.

Scala, M. (2001). *Working together Reading and writing in inclusive classrooms.* Newark, DE: International Reading Association.

Schwartz, S., & Bone, M. (1995). *Retelling, relating and reflecting.* Toronto, ON: Irwin.

Short, K. & Pierce, K, K. (1990). *Talking about books: Creating literate communities.* Toronto, ON: Irwin.

Sousa, D. (1995). *How the brain learns.* Reston, VA: NASSP.

Stauffer, R. (1970). *The language approach to teaching reading*. New York: Harper & Row.

Swartz, L. (1999). "The best response to a story is another story." In *Orbit*, Volume 30, Number 3.

Swartz L. (1993). *Classroom events through poetry*. Markham, ON: Pembroke Publishers.

Teale, W. (1982). "Assessing young children's literacy development: Wherefores, wheretos, whereins." Paper presented at the IRA Pre-convention Institute #26, Anaheim, CA, May 3–4, 1982.

Trelease, J, (1982). *The new read-aloud handbook*. New York: Penguin.

Vacca,R.T., & Vacca, J.L. (1989). *Content area reading (3rd Ed.)* New York: Harper Collins.

Vygotsky, l.S. (1988). *Thought and language*. Cambridge, MA: MIT Press.

Wells, G. (1986). *The meaning makers, children learning language and using language to learn*. Portsmouth, NH: Heinneman.

Wells, G., & Chang-Wells, G. (1992). *Constructing knowledge together: Classrooms as centres of inquiry and literacy*. Portsmouth, NH: Heinemann.

Wells, G. (1999). *Dialogic inquiry towards a socio-cultural practice and theory of education*. Cambridge, UK: Cambridge University Press.

Wlodkowski, R. (1985). *Enhancing adult motivation to learn*. San Fransisco, CA: Jossey Bass.

Zola, M. (1998). "Passing on the words." In *Orbit*:, Volume 28, No. 4, 30–33.

Children's Literature Cited

Blake, Q. (1994). *The Puffin Book of Nonsense Verse*. Toronto, ON: Puffin.

Blume, J. (1985). *The Pain and the Great One*. New York: Dell.

Bouchard, D. (1991). *My Little Pigs*. Winnipeg, MN: Whole Language Consultants.

Bouchard, D. (1997). *The Elders Are Watching*. Vancouver, BC: Raincoast Books.

Brett, J. (1985). *Armadillo Rodeo*: Boston, MA: Houghton Mifflin Company.

Brett, J. (2001). *Comets Nine Lives*. New York: Penguin.

Brown, M. (1989). *What's So Funny, Ketu?* NY: Penguin.

Carle, E. & Martin Jr., B. (1992) *Brown Bear, Brown Bear, What Do You See?* New York: Henry Holt and Company.

Cole, B. (1992). *Tarzania*. New York: Putnam and Sons.

Cole, J. (1991). *Eentsy, Weentsy Spider: finger plays and action rhymes*. New York: Morrow and Company.

Dahl, R. (1970) *Fantastic Mr. Fox*. New York: Bantam.

Dickenson, R. (1996). *The 13 Nights of Halloween*. New York: Scholastic

Durell, A., Craighead G. J., & Paterson, K. (1993). *The Big Book for Our Planet*. New York: Dutton.

Fleischman, P. (1988). *Joyful Noise: poems for two voices*. New York: Dell.

Foster, J. (2000). *Pet Poems*. Oxford, UK: Oxford University Press.

Fowke, E. (1978). *Sally Go Round the Sun*. Toronto, ON: McClelland and Stewart.

Gregory, N. (1995). *How Smudge Came*. Alberta: Northern Lights.

Hall, D. (1988). *Ox-cart man*. New York: Scholastic.

Hargreaves, R. (1976). *Mr. Jelly*. London, UK: Thurman Publishing Ltd.

Heidbreder, R. ((1985). *Don't Eat Spiders*. Oxford, UK: Oxford University Press.

Knowles, S. (1998). *Edward Emu*. New York: Harper Trophy.

Lee, D. (1974). *Alligator Pie*. Toronto, ON: Macmillan.

Lionni, L. (1989). *Swimmy*. New York: Scholastic.

Mayer, M. (1968). *There's a Nightmare in my Closet*. New York: Penguin.

MacLachlan, P. (1983). *Through Grampa's Eyes*. Toronto, ON: Fitzhenry & Whiteside.

MacLachlan, P. (1985). *Sarah, Plain and Tall*. New York: Harper & Row.

Meddaugh, S. (1992). *Martha Speaks*. New York: Houghton Mifflin.

Moore, L. (1970). *Spooky Rhymes and Riddles*. New York: Scholastic.

Numeroff, L. (1985). *If you give a mouse a cookie*. New York: Scholastic.

Pearlman, J. (1992). *Cinderella Penguin or, the little glass flipper*. Toronto, ON: Kids Can Press.

Pretlutsky, J. (1990). *Something big has been here*. New York: Scholastic.

Rathmann, P. (1991). *Ruby the Copy cat*. New York: Scholastic.

Reid, B. (1990). *Effie*. Toronto, ON: Scholastic.

Rylant, C. ((1995). *Dog Heaven*. New York: The Blue Sky Press.

Rylant, C. (1982). *When I was young in the mountains*. New York: E. B. Dutton.

Scieszka, J. (1989). *The true story of the three little pigs*. New York: Penguin.

Sendak, M. (1962). *Chicken Soup with Rice*. New York: Scholastic.

Silverstein, S. (1981). "Ation." *A Light in the Attic*. Hew York: HarperCollins.

Steig, W. (1991). *Amos & Boris*. New York: Scholastic.

Trivizas, E. (1994). *The three little wolves and the big bad pig*. New York: Scholastic.

Van Allsburg, C. (1985). *The Polar Express*. Boston, MA: Houghton Mifflin.

Viorst, J. (1983). *Alexander and the terrible, horrible, no good, very bad day*. Toronto, ON: McClelland & Stewart.

Yoshi, A. (1991). *Big Al*. Toronto, ON: Scholastic.

Zola, M. (1990). *Poetry Plus. Collections 2*. Toronto, ON: Copp Clark Pitman.

Index